Arian

Christian

Doctrines

(The origins of Christianity)

Written and Published by:
The Institute for Metaphysical Studies Inc

Other books by the Institute of metaphysical Studies Inc

An Alternate View of Reality

The Arian Christian Bible

Editor/Charles D. Levy, Director, Institute for Metaphysical Studies Inc

Copyright ©2010 Institute for Metaphysical Studies Inc
All rights reserved
Printed in the USA

ISBN 1-45376-461-5
EAN 978-1-45376-461-9

Introduction

The word 'Arian' should not be confused with the word 'Aryan', which is derived from Hindu philosophy and was inaccurately used by the German, NAZI party as the basis for its racist and anti-Semitic philosophy. The word 'Arian' was derived from the name of Saint Arius of Alexandria (in Egypt).

Although the word was derived from the name of St Arius, the word 'Arian" was coined by the Catholic Church as a pejorative name designed to define the heresy of those Christians who did not accept the Roman Catholic concept of the Holy Trinity and the divinity of Jesus. The term was used against those who would think for themselves.

This book is an attempt to right the record and bring back to Christianity the broad range of views that prevailed before the Romans co-opted the Christian Religion and turned it into a political arm of the Roman Empire.

St Arius' fame arose from his opposition to and disagreement with the results of the first Council of Nicaea, located in present day Turkey, which established the theological basis of Roman Catholic Christianity and the majority of the protestant churches that evolved in opposition to the Catholic religious hegemony. The result of this council was the conversion of Christianity from a personal non-political religion based on compassion and social tolerance into the political, national (State) religion of the Roman Empire.

3

St Arius' fame arose from his opposition to the results of the First Council of Nicaea, in modern day Turkey, convened by Constantine I, which established the theological basis of Roman Catholic Christianity. The result of this council was the conversion of Christianity from a religion of compassion, peace and personal spirituality into a political religion.

The Politics of Religion

Of the five great world religions, Buddhism and Christianity were founded as compassionate religions who purpose was the welfare of ordinary people caught up in the uncertainty, unpredictability and suffering that has afflicted men and women since the dawn of time.

The other three word religions, Islam, Hinduism, Judaism are political religions in the sense that the main objects of these religions are the wellbeing of a particular state, a particular culture a particular social structure and a particular nation or a particular place on the face of the Earth said to be special or holy.

In Judaism, a religion with roots going back at least 3000 years provided the basis for Christianity and Islam. In Judaism the main scripture, the Holy Scriptures[1] is primarily a political, cultural and religious history of the Jewish people and the State of Israel.

However, the Jewish religion did not begin as a political religion. The beginning of the transformation of Judaism into a political religion began with the ascendency of the Prophet Moses. The impact of Moses on Judaism, Islam and Christianity has been one of the most important events in human history. His impact was profound, but not surprising. Before the Exodus of the Jews

---

[1] Equivalent to the Old Testament in the Catholic Bible.

from Egypt, Moses was a prominent Egyptian politician and a consultant to the Pharaoh. Although he was a Jew, he was found, as a baby, floating among the reeds of the Nile river by an Egyptian Princess who adopted him and brought him up as an Egyptian nobleman. He was well versed in the political traditions of the Egyptian State and its use of religions as a means of congealing the government, the people, the religion and the military into one coherent political whole.

As Moses became aware of his Jewishness and the plight of his fellow Jews who were at that time suffering as Egyptian slaves, He became the champion of Jewish Emancipation. The Old Testament story is that through Devine intervention, Moses engineered the release of the Jews from captivity. After crossing the Red Sea, and finding himself stranded in the Sinai Desert with thousands of disrespectful and unruly Jews who questioned his leadership and intentions, Moses sought a solution to this primarily political problem.

The solution that Moses produced was brilliant, a stroke of genius, formulated from his background as an Egyptian politician. Since no one went up on the mountain with Moses and observed what happened, we have only have Moses' word, the word of a politician about what transpired and we will never know the truth except through faith.

What we do know, if we accept the account of the Old Testament, without having to rely on what Moses said happened on the mountain, is that Moses came down the mountain with two things, a stone tablet containing the Ten Commandments and a story about how he came to acquire the tablet. The story, essentially, was that God was the head of the State of Israel and was committed to its welfare and He had sent the tablet with rules of conduct, which, if followed, would lead to the existence of that state. Whether or not God gave the tablet to Moses or if he acquired it through another method is something that can never be known, since there were no witnesses. It is not important in this narrative, because for whatever reasons Moses did what he did, it worked. The religion of Judaism was restructured into a political religion with political goals structured for the benefit of the Jewish people. (The Jews who followed Moses out of slavery were not all of the Jewish people. The Falashas of Ethiopia and the Samaritans were Jews who had not been enslaved and did not practice the same rituals such as Yom Kippur or the Passover that were developed after the Exodus, and they did not have the same political goals as the Mosaic Jews who formed the State of Isr

Hinduism is also a political, cultural religion although their political and cultural structure is more diffuse that in Western religions. The Hindu caste system is the center of gravity of the Hindu political and cultural system. Their caste system consists of four rigidly defined casts or occupational groups. At the top are the Brahmins or religious class of priests and religious leaders. The next caste is that of the Kshatryas, which consists of political leaders and the military. The third caste is those families and groups who conduct and own businesses. The fourth and lowest class is the Sudras or laborers and employees. The rest the people called Dalats or the 'outcaste', who were mainly defined by skin color. These dark skinned Dravidians were deemed 'untouchable' by the lighter skinned 'Aryan' caste members of the four 'in casts'. (This counts in large for the hundreds of millions of 'untouchable' Hindus who converted to Islam because the Moguls (Mongol) Empire treated them as equals during their occupation of India.

Islam is the most political of the major religions. (The term 'political' is used as a descriptive term rather than as a pejorative one.) Mohammad is, without a doubt, the most important Arab who has ever lived. He was, first and foremost, a brilliant statesman, a political leader, a military leaded and a religious leader and a bringer of the laws. He was perhaps one of the most versatile humans who ever lived, even though he was illiterate. Islam makes no bones about its political nature.

Muhammad could easily see the advantage that the Jews and Christians of the Seventh century AD had over the Arabs based on the strength of their religious systems. Based on his view of the needs of the Arab people, Mohammad decided that the Christians got it wrong. That is to say, that Mohammad thought that the Christians had misinterpreted Judaism and that the Jews were just miscreants who had lost God's favor in favor of Muslims. Mohammad felt that the rule based Judaic system was much superior to Christianity for Arabs. Mohammad's objectives were the establishment of political and social stability for the Arab or Muslim world, which is called the Uma. Islam gained its aggressive evangelical nature from its observations of Christianity.

There are two reasons why the political nature of religion is emphasized versus religion's compassionate nature. These two natures are mutually incompatible. The tradecrafts of politics are deception, intrigue and war, which is an extension of diplomacy. The tools of compassionate religion are introspection and tolerance on an individual level.

In politically based religious systems, the individual gains value and benefit as byproduct of submitting to the rules of the religion as dictated by scripture and the dictates of the religion's priesthood and leaders.

The other two major religions are Christianity and Buddhism, which are both evangelical religions and reach out for converts as a matter of principle. Both religions are based on the premises of tolerance, compassion and peace. This is the way Christianity began.

The importance of Roman Emperor, Constantine I in the establishment and direction of modern Christianity cannot be overstated. As Roman Emperor, his opinions and desires were the same as laws. The confluence of Constantine I and Christianity brought a profound effect to both the Roman Empire and the Christian faith. This alignment of causes was fundamental to the development of western culture.

Constantine, like most dictators, liked order, orthodoxy and well defined social and political structures with strong unified leadership at the top. Because of the struggles he had endured in solidifying his hold on the reigns of Roman power, he disliked controversy and internal conflict that might lead to schism and opposition.

In 316 AD he led an army against a Christian Sect called the Donatists. For the first time in history, one set of Christians used military (political) power to crush dissidence within the Christian community. What Constantine I wanted was a church that reflected his own views regarding the structure of the Roman Empire. He wanted a Christian national religion that had one leader, one standard theology and one Church that was in accord with the political goals of the Roman Empire. To this end, he summoned the leaders of the Christian church to Nicaea in 325 AD, in present day Turkey, to deal with the heresy of Arianism. (The belief that Jesus was a man, or more importantly from a Catholic point of view, rejection of the principle that God was composed of three aspects of Father, Son and Holy Ghost) The problem posed by Jewish Christians whose allegiance to Jerusalem instead of Rome, as the center of gravity of Christianity was also perceived as a threat. The third major issue considered at the council of Nicaea was the problem of Gnosticism, which held that individuals could have a direct relationship with God or Jesus without the intervention of priests.

Apologists for the Politicized Catholic Church deny that Constantine I had a role in the edicts rendered by the Council of Nicaea in 325 AD. However, the primary desire of the officials of the church that convened in Nicaea was for the Christian Church to become the official state church of the Roman Empire. They were the supplicants, not Constantine I. There is no way they could have forced their views on the Roman Empire. They got what they wanted by submitting to the criticism and wishes of Constantine I. Later as the Roman Empire weakened and the Roman Catholic Church grew more powerful the equation changed dramatically. There was a quid pro quo. The church got official status and Rome got a subservient church.

Arianism and the Roman Catholic Church

The terms 'Arian' and 'Arianism' are words coined by the Roman Catholic Church and used by the Orthodox Churches and those Protestant churches whose theologies are based on the Roman Catholic Church, to denote the religious crime of heresy. According to these churches, Arianism is by definition heretical.

The question is for us who are Arian Christians is, "Why is Arianism a heretical practice?"

To examine this question we have to look at the history of the Roman Catholic Church and its political and religious belief structure. Although Jesus designated Simon, called peter, as the rock upon which his church would be established, the true founder of the Roman Catholic Church was Roman Emperor Constantine I.

The purpose of religion is to free men and women from suffering and to free their spirits and provide a connection to the divine. The purpose of political religions is to further the political, social interests of their founders with regard to specific cultural, national and social groups such as Jews and Israel, Muslims and the World Caliphate, and Hindus and their social structure. Political religions enslave their members to doctrines and scriptures said to be Holy, whose goal are the welfare of the religion and the State to the detriment of the spiritual welfare of its adherents.

Muhammad, Moses and Constantine I were politicians, and like all politicians they saw the world through the eyes of a politician in term of statehood for its people or nation. They used religion as a tool to enhance their respective political entities, Israel, Islamic theocracy and in the case of Constantine I, the Roman Empire. They adapted indigenous cultural and religious practices and the concept of Monotheism to advance their political objectives of nation building.

With specific regard to the influence of Constantine I, there would never have been a Roman Catholic[2] Church, or Orthodox churches or any of the present day Protestant churches. The future form of Christianity would have been completely different.

Constantine was born in what is now the country called Serbia in the year 372 AD. He became one of several co-Emperors of the Roman Empire in 306 AD. In 324 AD, he became the sole Roman Emperor until his death in 337 AD.

Not a lot is known about the personal life of Constantine I and it is not our intention to judge him. What we do know about him is that he was a Roman Emperor and as such, he was probably the most powerful man in the world with much greater powers than all but a few other dictators. What we do know is how the Roman Empire operated and what it did to other people in order to fill its coffers and enrich its citizens with slave and

---

[2] Catholic means 'Universal'

booty from its conquests. It sought to conquer, dominate and enslave every nation or cultural group that it came into contact with. Rome accomplished its ends through the efforts of a highly disciplined military and a political shrewdness that it used to divide and conquer, pitting brother against brother. After victory, they set up puppet regimes that collect taxes for Rome. Although the Romans advanced the technical culture of the people they oppressed, everyone hated them because they were tenacious, ambitious and merciless in the pursuit of conquest and power.

This is the system that Constantine I controlled and was controlled by. He was what we would now call a 'company man'. The Roman Emperors were so powerful that some of them actually believed that they were gods. One Emperor even went as far as having a man whisper in his ear whenever he went out into public, "Remember, you are not a god".

Constantine was the first Christian Emperor, and is considered as a Saint in the Eastern Orthodox Church and has the title "The Great" in the Latin or Roman Catholic Church. He rose through the ranks, serving in the Balkans, Persia, Britain, Gaul, Spain and Italy.

Although he was not born a Christian, he was an opponent of Christian persecution. Because of his military skills, he became one of the Roman co-Emperors. In 313 AD, he passed the Edict of Milan, along with his co-Emperor, Licinius, which outlawed Christian persecutions that had been in effect under the previous Emperor, Diocletian. The level of Constantine's commitment to Christianity has always been a subject of conjecture; He retained the title of Pontifex Maximus until his death as head of the pagan priesthood.

Constantine's conversion to Christianity is said to have begun when he had a vision, in 312 Ad, just before a battle with one of his opponents for leadership of the Roman Empire.

Arianism[3]

As discussed previously, Arianism has different meanings to different people. To the Catholic/Protestant point of view, Arianism is a many-faceted heresy that applies to all who dispute the Trinitarian[4] view.

Comparing Arianism to Trinitarianism is like comparing apples and oranges. The Trinitarian view is political view structured with the object of unifying Christianity into a single theology within a single unified Christian church with a structured clerical hierarchy, within the Roman Empire. With this formula, Jesus was elevated to a level that is equal to God. In a single stroke, Jesus, like God, becomes inaccessible to the common person, except through intervention of the priesthood.

The initial problem with the Trinitarian view is that the Trinitarian view is a negotiated compromise. Judaism is opposed to any such departmentalization of God into various parts. The cry of Israel is, "The Lord, Our God is One". There is nothing in Jesus' teaching or spoken words that mandates such a division. The purpose of the Trinitarian view was to elevate Jesus to a level where discussion of his humanity or level of divinity becomes impossible. Since Jesus is God, any discussion of his possible humanity or general divinity becomes heresy and therefore subject to political action by the Roman Empire, the defenders of the national faith.

---

[3] A summary of the history of Arianism is included in the appendix on page...

[4] The Trinitarian view is that God is composed of three co-equal named, "the Father, The Son And the Holy Ghost".

15

The questions posed by Arius of Alexandria, the Gnostics and the Jewish Christians were a serious threat to Roman hegemony. The First Ecumenical Council at Nicaea set the groundwork for the exclusion of Gnostic beliefs that men could have a one-to-one relationship with God or Jesus. It set the stage for the excommunication of all Arian Christians and others who refused to accept the Nicene Creed[5] as the basic definition of who and what a 'real' Christian was. By changing the Sabbath from Saturday to Sunday, they separated the Jewish Christians from the Gentile Christians. On the one hand, the Roman Church appropriated the Jewish Holy Scriptures and on the other hand, they vilified the Jew as the 'killers of Jesus.', when it was the Romans who actually did the physical deed of killing The Christ. The Jewish Christians were suppressed, scapegoated and subjected to pogroms until they were literally eliminated.

---

[5] See Appendix, page

The Arian Doctrines

The Arian doctrines, without the Trinitarian propaganda are simple and straightforward. They reflect the broad reach of the original Christianity taught by Jesus of Nazareth. Although most modern Protestant churches do not profess the same attitudes as the original 2nd century Catholic Church, the modern Protestant churches used the 2nd century Roman Catholic Church as the model upon which their theologies were based. Without the advantage of knowledge detailed knowledge of the formation of the Trinitarian Church, they did the best that they could. The most important and uniform Protestant change was the elimination of the political head of the church, the Papacy. What they did was like a man picking up a piece of meat from the ground and eating it without first wiping it off and examining it.

The Arian Doctrines, from an Arian viewpoint are as follow.

1. The Highest teachings of Christianity are contained in the words of Jesus the Christ as reported in the New Testament as reported by the Apostles Matthew, Mark and Luke.
2. Those reported words contain the totality of Jesus' teachings and the basis of Christianity and Christian theology.
3. The purposes of Jesus' teachings are compassionate and not political
4. The purpose of all scripture is to serve men to free men, and to widen their spiritual horizons and understanding.

5. The purpose of political religions is to enslave Man to scripture for religious, political and cultural purposes under the leadership of other men who are no different from any other men.

6. Each and every man has as much right to interpret the teachings presented in the words of Jesus Christ as any other man.

7. Moses, Constantine I and Muhammad all hijacked a religious process and converted it into a political process, in accord with their own political natures, for the benefit of their own cultural, national and social agendas, in the form Israel and the Jewish People, Rome and the Catholic Church, and the Arabs and the Islamic Caliphates. Each of these Politico-religions has at the center of their systems a piece of territory that they consider holy political ground, Such as Jerusalem, Rome, Mecca and Medina.

8. Arian Christianity is the expression of the original teachings of Jesus, which is humanist, compassionate, tolerant and peaceful.

9. Anyone who embraces Jesus' principles of the Golden Rule[6] as the guiding principle of his or her life is an Arian Christian, regardless of whether the belong to a church or not, regardless of whether they attend church, regardless of whether they are agnostic, Buddhist, Muslim, secular or even Atheist.

10. Jesus' teachings are available to all men and women.

---

[6] Do unto other as you would have them do unto you.

For a political religion, it is an easy matter to take a set of scripture or arguments and simply say that they are true or more likely, to say that the scriptures and arguments are 'The Word of God' and then use the power of the state and the religion to enforce that point of view. Political religions, because they are allied with the state can enforce its decrees through laws, military power and through economic pressures and enticements. The state can use its power to suppress contrary views.

For Arian Christians there is no such luxury of defining the truth by fiat. It must be done the hard way, through study and reflection. Reading the words of Jesus as recorded by his apostles is the key to understanding Jesus' teachings. If you have not read Jesus' words, then you cannot understand his teachings. In the passage of our lives we will, most of us, experience pain and suffering, loss and victory, love and hate; these are common experiences. Unlike political religions, Jesus tells us that we should give to 'Caesar things that are Caesar's and to God those things that belong to God'. He is telling us that there are two aspects to our lives. The first aspect is the aspect of Caesar in that we are under the influence of human, historical, economic, military, environmental powers that affect our lives. These are the secondary powers. The primary power is that power that Jesus describes in a very controversial way. Jesus calls this primary power, 'My Father in Heaven', and 'Our Father in Heaven'. In his wisdom and compassion, he never describes what or who God is. He calls himself, "the Son of man', He tells us that the 'Kingdom of Heaven is within us' and for Arians it is an easy matter to deduce that if the Kingdom of

Heaven is within us, then that is where God is also. To the Trinitarians and the Political Christians, this is heresy, because they say so. However, the truth of the matter is obvious to anyone who examines his or her experiences and feelings. Everything that we experience and feel, we feel within, inside of us. Happiness, love, hate, fear, pain and suffering are affairs that we can never share with others except through their empathy of compassion.

The central unifying factor and belief of Arianism is that Jesus is not God. For some Arians, Jesus is a divine being, for some he is the Messiah, for some he might be the Son of God, for others he was a human being no different from any other human being, with abilities that are known and accessible to all men. To some he was a man who, knowing his destiny, accepted his fate, aware of his humanity, with a dignity and command that is worthy of emulation.

Each Christian owes it to himself to ask the question, "Was Jesus a man or a God?" What is the probability that Jesus was God and did not speak directly to that matter? Did Jesus lie when he called himself the 'Son of Man'? What are our own experiences with regard to life and death and the finality of its outcome? The answers to these questions are in the words of Jesus in the Gospels of the New Testament, and no place else. There are many who are satisfied by the convenient truths imposed on Christianity by Constantine I. Arian Christians are not satisfied by this kind of truth.

Because Arian Christianity involves internal processes of knowledge, it is no more possible to write out a detailed, static doctrine than it is to write a doctrine on love or a definition of God that satisfies everyone. This leads us to a discussion of perhaps the most important aspect of all religions. That is faith. Faith is an extraordinary ability that all people have in varying degrees. Faith is by definition a lack of knowledge about something or someone. It is the subjective ability to accept as true or not true: that which may or may not be true. Without faith we would be lost, we would have to figure out the possibilities and probabilities for each act we perform. We would not be able to make decisions or take action in the face of the unpredictability of the future.

Actually, faith is not a specifically religious power, when we flip a light switch we have faith that the light will go on. If it does not, we look for the reason why; is there a power outage, is the lamp plugged in, is the fuse burned out, is the bulb burned out. We do not pray to God for a solution. However, when we are suffering or uncertain about the future, we believe, according to our faith, in the Old Testament God in the Sky, in the Bible, in Jesus, In the God within, in ourselves.

Even Atheists have faith, even though they would deny it. Belief in 'no God', or disbelief in a particular definition of God, or belief in God or in a particular description of God is a matter of faith. Atheists can give arguments against the existence of God, but no proof. They call on science, but Science only deals with physical phenomena. Atheists have faith in their gut feelings and will defend those feelings as a matter of faith, even though they cannot provide 'scientific' proof that their views are correct.

Faith is central to Arian Christianity, and all religions and political systems. However, if we place our faith in the wrong things, we will suffer the consequences. Jesus tells us that we should accommodate ourselves to those things that are of Caesar's political world, but we should not place our faith in that world, but in God's world, which is found within.

Politicians and political religions are interested in money, power, and control, national and cultural interests and the use of deception and military actions to gain those ends.

Jesus, Muhammad, the Buddha, Constantine I and Moses understood the power of faith and its ability to motivate people. The most important question for Arian Christians is, "In what or whom should I place my faith?"

Fortunately, for Arian Christians there is a starting point that can used to address this question. We have a Bible that was assembled by Christian scholars in as reasonable, logical and earnest fashion as they could. The Books of the Bible are arranged in a historical/authentic hierarchy of importance that reflects the importance of the teachings of Jesus of Nazareth in the form of his words as recanted by his apostles in the New Testament.

The Bible is divided into two parts, the Old Testament and the New Testament.

The Old Testament is recorded in historical order from Genesis to Malachi. The Old Testament is two thirds of the Bible in number of pages. The Jewish Holy Scriptures runs from Genesis through Second Chronicles and is about the same length as the Christian Holy Bible.

The Old Testament and the Jewish Holy Scriptures are a chronological history of the Jewish people, the State of Israel, its laws and customs and culture. The modern Jewish State and culture are organized around this scripture. These are books for the Jews and those who wish to follow the Jewish culture and lifestyle.

The Christian scholars who compiled the Bible put the Jewish Holy Scriptures first because they happened first. They were not placed first because they were the highest and important teachings of Jesus or Christianity. Quite to the contrary, the Old Testament scriptures were added as a contrast to the New Testament and the new revolutionary teachings of Jesus of Nazareth.

The Old Testament was not included in the Bible as an equal partner with the New Testament, but as a contrast of old and new, of inferior (from a Christian viewpoint) teachings to inferior teachings. The Old Testament was included as an honored foundation, as a historical necessity. Most of the Roman, Gentile Christian hierarchy held the Jews in contempt, considered their teachings as inferior, and accused them of being Christ killers.

Constantine I said of the Jews, _"... it appeared an unworthy thing that in the celebration of this most holy feast we should follow the practice of the Jews, who have impiously defiled their hands with enormous sin, and are, therefore, deservedly_ *afflicted with blindness of soul. ... Let us then have nothing in common with the detestable Jewish crowd; for we have received from our Savior a different way.* "[7]

However, after suppressing the Christian Jews from Christian membership, the Romans used the Old Testament as a base because of its political content and its usefulness to Roman political aims. Because the Old Testament and the New were combined, and are contradictory to each other, it allowed great leeway in interpreting the combined scriptures in any way that the Romans and Roman Church wished.

Jesus said that he had not come to destroy the (Jewish) scriptures, but to change the importance of the scriptures to the lives of everyday people. Large parts of Jesus' teachings are about the hypocrisy of how the Jewish clergy use the scriptures to their advantage to cheat and mislead the common people. He said that, 'The scriptures are meant to serve men and not the other way around.'

This is one of the revolutionary differences between Christianity and Judaism (and Islam and the Koran, which came later.)

The Old Testament contains a voluminous list of laws and rules regarding everyday life that obligated the ordinary Jew to the Priesthood and the Jewish Government. Muhammad and Islam copied this Jewish, ruled based theology in order to control the Arab masses. (This is why Muhammad said that the Christians

---

[7] Eusebius, *Life of Constantine* Vol. III Ch. XVIII Life of Constantine (Book III)

"got it wrong'. (That is, the Christians did not understand the political part of Judaism.)

Jesus presented his ideas and teachings as a set of concepts, rather than static rules, which addressed the dignity and worth of each individual and his or her relationship to that which a person considers God, rather than a relationship to a set of words or a country or a culture. He taught of forgiveness rather than revenge and tolerance rather than judgment.

Admittedly, this is not a popular view. Most Catholic, Orthodox and Protestant Christians believe that the Old and the New Testaments are equal without giving much thought to it either way, after all they are parts of the same book. Muslims, fundamentalist Christians and Jews, of course, think the Old Testament is superior to the New Testament.

Closer examination of some of the differences will show that the principle of the Old Testament and the New Testament diverge in form and content and spirit.

The Old Testament says that women who are adulterous and homosexuals should be stoned to death. The New Testament says, "Do unto others as you would have them do unto you". The Old Testament says, 'an eye for an eye and a tooth for a tooth!', but Jesus said, 'Turn the other cheek. Faced with either of these situations it should be obvious to all Christians as to the preferred line of action. Jesus also said, 'He who lives by the sword shall die by the sword'. Many people who call themselves Christians would have a problem turning the other cheek in the wake of an assault, but this strategy has powerful moral weight and reflects deep, long term, wisdom.

The American civil rights movement and the Indian liberation movement relied on moral pressure and non-violent resistance. One of the many reasons of the ascendancy of the Western nation states after the Protestant Reformation was the waning of power of the Holy Roman Church, as Christianity was reformed. The relative submission of the various protestant Churches and their lack of political drive and unity allowed powerful, secular nation states to arise in northern Europe and North America. These states are strong because they are not subject to the whims and political leadership of a self- ordained clergy. One can contrast these states with the plight of Catholic dominated countries in South America and the states of the Islamic world. The power of the clergy in the Islamic nations is such that there is a constant struggle between the government and the clergy for control of the direction of those nations. In these states, the clergy fights to go backward or to maintain the status quo. This is a major reason for the political and economic backwardness of most Islamic nation states. Usually what happens is that a strong man takes control of the reins of power as a virtual dictator. Other than the small, oil rich Gulf Emirates, Turkey is the only Islamic country approaching the economic vibrancy of the West or the East. The reason for this is that Turkey has deliberately suppressed the political power of the Islamic clergy.

The Bible, the Old Testament, the New Testament and the Gospels of the Apostles.

To the true Christian, the only place that he or she should look is to the New Testament. The only question is, "Where in the New Testament should I look?"

The Bible can be likened to a pile of rocks that contain a few gem quality stones, a diamond, a ruby and an emerald, many more semi-precious stones and finally a lot of pebbles of little value. To the non-discerning mind, the whole pile of rocks has the same value. The rock pile is valued because it is said to have something of great value within it.

To the discerning mind, the diamond, the ruby and the emerald are the Gospels of Matthew, Mark and Luke. The semi-precious stones are the other books of the New Testament and the pebbles are the Old Testament.

Again, the Christian scholars who compiled the Jewish Holy Scriptures and the New Testament into the Holy Bible did so with regard to time, but books of the New Testament were deliberately placed in order with regard to authenticity, veracity, concurrence and believability.

First, they put the four Gospels of the recollections of Matthew, then Mark, then Luke and last John. Next, came the Acts of the Apostles, then the letters of the Apostles to the various Greek congregations and finally the visions in Revelations, which appeared to the Apostle John.

The reason why Matthew, Mark and Luke are first and John is the last of the four Gospels, which claim to report the words of Jesus, is because the Gospel of John is of a different caliber and authenticity than the first three.

The first three are generally are generally coherent and supportive of one another. They seem to be the experiences of people who consider themselves Jews, as were Jesus' original followers. On the other hand, John seems to have been written by a Gentile who had little knowledge of Jewish traditions and who expressed on openly anti-Semitic point of view that would have been common to gentiles of that era. John did not even know that Samaritans were a sect of pre-Mosaic Jews, such as modern day Falashas of Ethiopia, who did not experience the exodus from Egypt.

It is fairly easy to discern the plan the Christian scholars of the 2nd century used in laying out the Bible. First the words of Jesus, second the acts and words of the Apostles and finally the Old Testament, as a contrast between the old and the new. This is the contrast between the superior New Testament and the flawed Old Testament. From the Christian point of the Old Testament is flawed because the Old Testament favors the Jews over all other men. The Old Testament claims a monopoly over the one Monotheistic God. Christians believe that God loves us all equally, regardless of circumstance, race, or nationality. Christianity is for all men, not just a select few, as in the Old Testament Judaism.

Admittedly, most Jews, Muslims and many Christians will disagree with this analysis. However, for Christians it should be a matter of faith that if there is any divergence between the Old Testament and the New Testament, that the New Testament should have precedence. In the New Testament, Matthew Mark Luke and John should have precedence over the acts and letters of the Apostles, and Matthew, Mark and Luke should have precedence over John because they are in accord with each other and John is not. Because it is first in the New Testament, Matthew probably has the greatest authenticity.

Thanks to the diligence and spiritual guidance given by the Christian monks and scholars used in compiling the Holy Bible, even though it was 300 years after Jesus' death, we have a relative scale with which we can weigh Jesus' teachings.

The Trinitarians backed up their arguments with the virtual bumper sticker, **"God said it, I believe it and that's the end of it"**. Although this is a perplexing statement, what this Constantinian view is really saying is, "I don't care about the facts, I don't care what others say, I don't care if I am right or wrong, this is my position and I will not change".

The First Ecumenical Council of Nicaea in 325 AD voted that God was composed of 'The Father, the Son and the Holy Ghost' by a vote of 318 to 2 votes against; this was ratified by Constantine I, who was the final arbiter of the councils' endeavors. Constantine I convened the council, with the purpose of suppressing dissent and discussion of the true nature of God and Christianity; he established a litmus test for all Christians in the form of the Nicene Creed.[8] It established the setting for the combination of the Jewish Old testament with the Christian New Testament in the Bible as documents of equal value.

One of the most pronounced differences between the Old and New Testament is that the Old Testament presents a chronology of the Universe that is at odds with science and common sense.

Most Muslims and many non-Arian Christians believe that the Universe is less than 10,000 years old. They believe that the Bible and the Koran, which are based on the Old Testament, are the words of God and therefore the literal truth. (They have no choice in taking this position. If one part of the Bible or Koran was found to be not the literal truth, then other parts might also be not true also, and so forth.) This point of view refutes the position of Archaeology, Astronomy, Biology, Geology and Physics.

The New Testament makes no such assertions about the origins of the universe, and the words of Jesus, wisely, do not touch on this subject. The Old Testament contains a complete, rule-based cosmology that attempts to explain the history of the universe with a simplistic story that might have allegorical value but is devoid of facts. This universe is much too complex and profound for such an explanation. The writers of the Old Testament were not concerned with science because science did not exist. Believers in the Old Testament are not concerned with science or any opinion or process that does not reflect the

---

[8] See appendix

literal words of the Bible, even though there are many different translations of the Bible. The goal of these believers is to present a worldview that is absolute, not relative and certain. It is view that presents a world that is stable and unchanging, a refuge for deniers of the observational fact that the actual world we live in is changing, relative and uncertain. The Old Testament and the Koran address these issues with thousands of rules and regulations about every aspect of life.

The teachings and words of Jesus of Nazareth address the world with situational concepts rather than rigid rules. These situational concepts allow ordinary people to resist the religious slavery to scripture and its clerical interpreters and politicians and hypocrites who would use religion to subvert their obligation to God by confusing them with the rewards of Mammon.

This is an argument that Jesus makes in his own words. It is not an attack on scripture, per se, but against those who would interpret scripture in such a way as to give advantage to themselves in manipulating the multitudes. This is why the Pharisees wanted Jesus killed. He called them out as hypocrites and deceivers of the masses.

Another difference is the difference between the Old Testament and the Koran and the New Testament, especially the Arian Gospels[9], the books of Matthew, Mark and Luke, is the issue of slavery. The Confederate States of America succeeded from the United States over slavery. The Bible, specifically the Old

---

[9] See Arian Bible in appendix.

Testament was used to validate their arguments about slavery. The Koran also supports slavery, although in a more benign manner.

The teachings of Jesus Christ directly oppose such treatment of other people. This conflict between the Old and New testament was fertile ground for clever and deceptive arguments that defended the moral degeneracy of slavery, and incited Christians to advocate violence and war to support the interest of wealthy Southern slaveholders.

Jesus did not counter these arguments with counter-arguments; he spoke to his followers about the motives of the scripture interpreters. He tells his followers to be different than they are and to be suspicious of them. He points out the power the wealthy and influential have to manipulate those who interpret scripture. He tells how the wealthy will sell their souls in order to acquire and maintain their wealth. (Jesus was killed because he challenged the authority of the wealthy and powerful.)

To a true Christian, to Arian Christians, the words and life of Jesus are enough to solve any problem life presents to us, He presents a clear practice of humility, honesty, simplicity tolerance, and openness of spirit and heart. He tells us that he is come to give solace and forgiveness to those of us ordinary people who are flawed and imperfect and suffering. He gave us the secret of eternal life, not through scripture or God but as a natural result of us just being alive in the first place. He taught us that the Kingdom of God is within us.

Then who are these Arian Christians? The Catholics and the Trinitarian Protestants say that the Arian Christians are Atheists, infidels, heretics and unbelievers. They say that the Arians live in sin and are deluded because they do not accept the Godhood of Jesus and the whole of the Bible as revealed truth. The Trinitarians say that their views are infallible, that the Bible is infallible and those who disagree with them (the Arians) are simply wrong and will be punished in Hell.

The point of these arguments is to suppress discussion of religion and the possibility that there might be errors in the revealed word.

Jesus did not argue the right or wrong of scripture, he talked about the effect that scripture had on ordinary people who were seeking an answer to the chaos and difficulties life presented; poverty, sickness, war and famine. He talked about those who would manipulate the scripture for their own benefit. He taught us, 'what is the value of money or power if it destroys our faith and our ability to believe in that which is right and just?'

How does a person know if he or she is an Arian Christian or not? If you have ever asked the question, "What would Jesus do?" you are probably an Arian Christian. Why would a person ask what Jesus would do as a personal guide, if they believed that Jesus was God? Who would ask what God would do as a resolution to a personal problem when ordinary people do not have the powers of gods?

Do you go to church? If not, is it because you are uncomfortable with the atmosphere of churches, but still you consider yourself a Christian. If this is the case, then you are probably an Arian Christian. Do you believe in the Old Testament God of vengeance, fire and brimstone; an Old Man in the sky? If not, you are probably an Arian Christian. If you believe that God is an un-manifest, indescribable being, but still believe you are a Christian, no matter what anyone else says, then you are probably an Arian Christian.

Are you an Atheist or a person with secular views who accepts the Golden Rule of 'Do unto others as you would have them do unto you' as a moral guide? Do you accept Jesus' moral, philosophical, guidelines without all the 'hocus pocus'? Do you consider yourself 'not' a Christian because others say that you are not? It should not matter, because it did not matter to Jesus.

If Jesus is God, then Jesus' teaching have no meaning because we are not gods and we would have no reference point to judge the value of his teachings. However, if Jesus is something less that God, a man such as the Messiah[10] or even the Son of God, or a human being in any form, divine or not, then we can form an opinion about his teachings because we have a reference point of our own humanity.

Even if Jesus is not God, his words and actions as reported is the only source we have. The Gospels of the New Testament have profound eloquence and meaning in themselves, without the

---

[10] See Appendix

support of any other religious or philosophical underpinning, except as a contrast. Jesus' words measure up to or surpass all the other scriptural or philosophical writings of the world.

If you believe that Jesus was human in any form, and not God, then you are, by definition, an Arian Christian.

If you believe in the Trinitarian view that Jesus is God, or a part of God in a way that is different from any ordinary person, or that Jesus was not the creation of God, or that the proper description and identity of God is, 'The Father, the Son and The Holy Ghost'. Then you must look to your priests and political religions for answers to your problems and questions, and pray that they will put your interests first.

For those Christians who are Arian Christians, it should be pointed out that before the Council of Nicaea all Christians were Arian Christians. There was no such thing as a Holy Trinity before this. The Council of Nicaea marked the bifurcation of Christianity into The Roman Catholic Church and Arian heretics. These Arians included Jewish Christians, Gnostic Christians and all other Christians who would not accept Constantine I's *fait accompli* with regard to the Christian Church.

Jesus never said that he was God or that he was part of any Holy Trinity. Jesus for the most part referred to himself as the Son of Man, When asked directly if he was the Son of God, he never answered the question, he said, "You say that I am.", or in response to the question from others he would say, "who do you think I am?

Jesus referred to God as his Father. How then, could Jesus be God? When Jesus taught us how to pray, he told us to say, "Our Father, who art in Heaven..." If he taught us to say that God is also our Father, how are we any different from him, except in the depth of his wisdom, which is an attribute many humans have.

Jesus never described who or what God is except in broad generalities, and rightly and wisely so. Many Protestant, fundamentalist Christians will say, "I know that there is a God". They say this without a true understanding of faith and the importance of faith in Jesus' teachings. They will even say that they 'know' God's thoughts and God's Plan. Because they lack humility and judgment, they are not at all concerned that God's thoughts are, imagine that, exactly the same as their own thoughts. They believe that God must be just like them and that their thoughts and feelings are the same as facts.

To be sure, faith is an ability that human beings possess. It is the ability to accept as true or untrue, that, which cannot be proven. These people do not understand that their personal feelings, gut feelings and anecdotal experiences are not proof.

Jesus teaches about the correct application of faith. He taught us that we should not throw the pearl of faith before swine, which means that faith without wisdom is foolishness. If a person has faith that he can fly, he would be wise to use an airplane, or if he wished to move a mountain, he would be well served to use his faith to get some bulldozers. The source of wisdom lies within that heart that is well regulated by a clear, calm and untroubled mind.

When people were healed in Jesus' presence, he told them that it was their faith that healed them. Did he lie? When people were raised from the dead, he said that they were sleeping. Did he lie? Jesus said that the Kingdom of Heaven is within us. Did he lie?

The early Christians did not accept Jesus as God. For Jews to do so would have been blasphemy and all of his early followers were Jews. This is an Arian point of view. Some accepted Jesus as the Son of God, some as the Messiah, some as a Rabbi, but none believed he was God. His family and neighbors refused to accept him as anything at all except as the son of Joseph and Mary. Some saw him as an extraordinary man.

Jesus and the Bible.

Constantine I, the Emperor of Rome, convened the Council of Nicaea to counter the influence of Arianism and Gnosticism. Gnosticism, in general, is the belief that men can establish a one-to one relationship with God without the need for the obligatory intercession of the priesthood, or even Jesus. (Jesus was considered the path and the way to a relationship with God but not God himself.)

Gnostics believed that Jesus taught that the Kingdom of heaven was within and God is therefore found within also. They believed that the process of creating a personal relationship with God was an internal and personal process that the church could not mediate. (The Trinitarian view is that one-to-one relationships are not possible without the mediation of the church and the clergy.

These points of view posed a threat to Constantine's desire for order, control, unity and conformity within the Church as the official Roman state religion, and to provide for the economic viability of the priesthood by forcing all Christians to have to pay the church for access to Jesus and God. This was the primary political goal of Constantine I. The Arians and Gnostics were excommunicated and then suppressed with vicious propaganda, peer pressure, economic discrimination, and warfare. The Jews and Christian Jews were subjected to pogroms.

It should be noted that the Roman Catholic Church was not the main cause of the heretical status of Arianism. The primary cause was the Roman Empire. The primary design of the Roman Empire and its Emperors was the conquest, subjugation and enslavement of all people and nations that they encountered. They conquered indiscriminately for booty, slaves and power. The Roman Caesars were dictators, lunatics and sadists. Christianity was just another process that they sought to pervert to their own ends.

The Christian church, the Catholic Church, the Arians, the Jews and the Gnostics were simply victims of Roman ambitions. The Catholic Church, after the fall of the Roman Empire, gradually adapted to a more 'Christian' relationship with other religions and groups. The Catholic Church, released from the control of the Romans, has shown the grudging ability to adapt and have a modicum of introspection and be more accessible to reason. Catholic universities are on a par with the best secular universities. The Church has come into agreement with mainstream science after a long and difficult struggle. The Church is even open to the idea that some parts of the Bible are allegorical; and has even entertained the idea that the 'Big Bang Theory' with regard to the origins of the universe. The Catholic Church has responded to criticism by adapting, because unlike the Roman Empire, it is not a power unto itself.

However, even as Catholicism has reformed itself, the fundamentalist Protestant movement has taken on the same rigidity of outlook and form as the medieval Catholic Church. Especially in America, there are Protestant sects that believe that the Bible is the absolute, literal word of God. (Muslims believe this also)

They believe that the world was created in 7 days. They believe that the primary cause of the chaotic nature of the human experience developed from a conversation between a woman and a snake about a magic apple.

Of course, this is a ludicrous story. The woman is the culprit who ruined the male of the species, and is the reason men must dominate women so as to keep their inherent evil in check. People who believe these Old Testament stories as absolute truth are not real Christian, but Judeo-Christians, or pseudo-Jews, or people who believe in Judaism but act as if they were Christians. They put the teachings and rules of the Old Testament before and above the New Testament and the words of Jesus. Their insistence on the literal truth of the Old Testament causes them to reject science, especially Geology, Astronomy, Biology and Archeology. It makes them reject anything that even remotely disagrees with Genesis and the literal truth of anything written in the Old Testament.

They reject and completely misunderstand Jesus' teachings and the original Arian basis of Christianity. It is impossible to explain any opposing viewpoint to them; they have extensive arguments that support their positions. Any contradiction to their position is simply an opportunity for them to express the strength of their faith.

The teachings of Jesus and Arian Christianity do not depend on how the world was created or how God created the world. The phrase, "Do unto others as you would have them do unto you". It is not dependent on any other external factors for vindication or understanding or its inherent wisdom. It is not dependent on what might happen to us in heaven or on some other future day. It is a simple statement of a moral truth. The world that Jesus taught about was not the world of death or heaven or Hell. It was about everyday life. It was about the moment-to-moment passage of our lives and our day-to-day connection to that which is good, tolerant, and loving of our neighbors and ourselves. Jesus explained how to live the everyday life of ordinary people who struggle to survive and keep their balance in a world of trial and circumstances that are not within our control. Jesus taught us; "Look at the birds in the sky, does God not feed and keep them? " Why should we worry about tomorrows' problems when there are enough problems for us to solve today?" If we are to die tomorrow, then the life we have lived up to today is important, but if tomorrow is given to us, then why not live it to the best of our ability without worry or regret?

Fortunately, we do have a starting point that we can use to reconstruct Jesus' teachings. If we eliminate the sources of conflict within the Bible that conflict with and contradict Jesus' teachings, the path to understanding is much simpler. Jesus' words, when confabulated with the Old Testament teachings, have a very different meaning when read outside of the context of the Old Testament, even though the words are the same.

If we eliminate the inferior sections of the Bible and Trinitarian theology such as:

1. The Old testament, which primarily reflects Jewish cultural and religious history.
2. The acts of the Apostles
3. Letters of the Apostles to the various Christian communities in Greece, such as Thessalonica and Corinth, which are commentaries on Jesus' words and works.
4. Roman Catholic political theology.

We can get a much better view of Jesus' teachings without these distractions.

Although it may seem that Jesus' words might seem to be contradictory at times, it should be taken into account that Jesus spoke with a different tone and on a different level according to whom he was speaking.

In general, Jesus communicated with four different types of people.

1. Disciples
2. The 'multitudes' or ordinary people.
3. The Pharisees and religious authorities.
4. Samaritans and gentiles.

Jesus spoke to his disciples with detail explanations of Jewish scripture and explanations of the parables he related to the multitudes. He spoke to the multitudes, the ordinary people in parables or descriptive stories. He spoke to the Pharisees about scripture and he admonished them and the religious leadership for their hypocrisy. He spoke bluntly to Samaritans and gentiles but praised them when they responded to him with wisdom and a show of faith.

As describe before, one of the most unfortunate things that the Roman Catholic Church did was to combine the Old and New Testament into one book, which we call the Holy Bible.

Judaism and Christianity are two different religions. Jews do not consider themselves to be Christians and Christians do not consider themselves to be Jews. The only real similarity is that they both call themselves Monotheists. The Jews did not invent Monotheism. They did not invent the first political religion. Judaism was the first Monotheistic religion that fashioned the One God into a God that favored a particular nation a particular culture and people, effectively outflanking any other western expression of Monotheism.

Jews, quite naturally, consider Judaism to be superior to Christianity, (and Islam for that matter) because the Jewish Holy Scriptures were written by Jews as a record of their religious, cultural and political history and these writings were appropriated by both the Muslims and Christians. Many Jews did not consider Jesus to be the Messiah, but just an ordinary Jew without significant religious credibility. The Jews are not at all pleased that that their scriptures and religion were taken and modified into an instrument that was used against them by both Christians and Muslims. Christians do not see this as a problem because they were not the victims. Muslims do not see it as a problem because they see Jews as miscreants.

Of course, there is no longer any significant community of Christian Jews anymore. Originally, Arian Christians co-existed with Jewish Christians until the Jewish Christians were suppressed and the Arian Christians declared heretics.

The reasons behind these actions against the Arians, Gnostics and Christian Jews were politically motivated. Suppose the verdict of the Council of Nicaea was decided 318 to 2 in favor of Arianism, instead of the other way around. Would that have meant that Jesus was not God?

The Trinity of God was based on a vote by men. Even if Arianism had won in the vote, Constantine I would not have accepted it.

The result of these events is that most Christians see the Old and New Testaments as presenting one continuous, homogenous Christian religion. Many fundamentalist Protestant Christians hold the Old Testament to be superior or at least equal to the New Testament. They believe that the Bible is the literal truth and keeping this 'original' truth intact is more important than any of Jesus' subsequent teachings were.

This dogmatic support of Old Testament theology is not supported by the actions and teachings of the original Christians, the Arians, or by modern mainstream Christianity. This subversion of Christianity to the 'no matter what' defense of Genesis misdirects and undermines the compassion and tolerance of Jesus' teachings. Jesus never spoke about the infallibility of Genesis or any other scripture, but about the fallibility of men who would misinterpret scripture to their own benefit.

The Arian Christians were the original Christians before the imposition of the accords of the First Ecumenical council of Nicaea in 325 AD, which brought the Christian church under the influence of the Roman Empire. The Doctrine of the 'Holy Trinity' which had the primary purpose of 'deifying Jesus, was not devised through divine revelation, but through the vote and deliberation of men and the consent of Constantine I, the most powerful man in the world.

Constantine I wanted a church that reflected the rigid hierarchy of the Roman Empire. Arians with their multiple opinions and disputes and Gnostics with their lack of need for the church were threats that did not fit into the Roman management model.

Who was Jesus?

Historically, the only evidence we have of the existence of Jesus are the oral accounts of Jesus' disciples Matthew, Mark, Luke and John which were originally written down in Greek two or three hundred years after Jesus' death.

Perhaps the most important question a Christian can ask, and one of the most important questions Arian Christians asked was, "Who was Jesus?" The Trinitarian view is that Jesus and God the Father and the Holy Ghost are all different aspect of one single undivided God. This Trinitarian view did not exist before the Council of Nicaea. Some Christians in that period believed that Jesus was the Son of God; Jewish Christians believed that he was the Messiah, some believed that he was possibly a divinely possessed human being, some believed he was a man. Some believed that Jesus' teachings were the gateway to a personal relationship to God.

In order to examine Jesus' teachings in detail we have to separate the Trinitarian distortions and the Old Testaments' lack of compatibility with science, from the original word of Jesus as presented to us in the Gospels of Matthew, Mark, Luke and even John's Trinitarian slant. In these books, we need to be aware of the audience Jesus to whom was speaking.[11]

When Jesus spoke to the multitudes, he spoke in parables that emphasized peacefulness, tolerance, introspection, humility and faith. He did not quote from scripture, but used stories that explained the basics of this philosophy.

When Jesus spoke to the Pharisees, scribes, and others of the Jewish clerical structure, he quoted scripture. He admonished them, with threats and insults, for committing the greatest of sins for which there was no repentance and that was the sin of hypocrisy. For all other sins he said, "Your sins are forgiven, go and sin no more". Hypocrisy in the clergy was singled out because hypocrisy undermines the faith of the hypocrite and those who would follow him. He challenged them because they strove to make others conform to scripture while they did the opposite, creating cynicism in the believers.

---

[11] The Gospels of the Apostles are paraphrased so that the reader will read the Gospels for themselves.

When Jesus spoke to Samaritan Jews or Gentiles, he spoke to them as equals, commending their wisdom when presented, and responded to their questions with wisdom when asked.

When he spoke to his disciples, he explained things in detail even though they often did not understand him.

To all he spoke of the importance of well placed-faith in him and his teachings.

What was Jesus' spoken relationship with God? For the most part, Jesus called himself, "The son of Man." He wisely never defined God, except as his 'Father in Heaven' and when asked how to pray, he said, we should pray to, "Our father in Heaven..."

When Jesus described God in terms of God's negative power and ability to punish, he was always speaking about and to the Jewish clergy, the Pharisees and Sadducees, Jewish religious factions.

Religious Authority

One of the most challenging questions Arian Christians brought forward was the question of 'authority' in regard to Christian theology. In the Roman model of Christianity that appeared after the Nicaean Council, the theological authority was lodged in the Roman Catholic Church, and the Roman Empire took on the responsibility of defending the Faith with all the political and military resources of the State.

Since Arianism is not a political religion, these political issues were not of concern. Arians followed Jesus' teaching with regard to accommodating political entities such as the Roman Empire, which was, as he stated, "Give unto Caesar that which belongs to Caesar, and to God those thing which belong to God".

In Christianity, the highest authority is the words of Jesus[12], as recorded in the New Testament in the books of Matthew, Mark, and Luke. Even John has greater authority than all of the other books of the Bible combined. Certainly, it is not the Jews and their personal scripture. It is not Constantine I. The Jews did not create their religion to please or define Christian theology. They created it, or it was given to them, for their own uses. If we are not scribes or Pharisees or the Jewish religious hierarchy, or followers of Constantine I, then Jesus', words about their hypocrisy are not for Arian Christians. The teachings to the Apostles are meant for apostles or those who would be apostles and celibate.

---

[12] 'Faith is gained by hearing and reading Jesus' words.'

For the most part Jesus' teachings are directed at those of us who are ordinary people.

The Churches and the clergy tell us that the Bible and the Koran are the word of God, and given to us by God, therefore who are we ordinary people to have any opinion about any of this when God has spoken and speaks to us through the clergy.

Who has authority over who is a Christian and who is not? I suggest that no man and no church has this authority. The original Arian Christians had no such procedure to determine who was a Christian and who was not. Baptism is not an indication of Christianity, but of intent and is not required of all Christians. It is acceptance of the 'meaning' of Jesus' words that makes us Christian. However, lack of faith does not mean that we are not Christians either. The only person who knows for certain if we are Christian or not is ourselves. It is not a matter of appearances; it is what is in our hearts that counts.

Jesus' teachings are contained in his words as reported in the Gospels, and his words are the only physical evidence we have of his teachings. The other thing that makes us Christians on a personal level is the appearance of Jesus in our lives as an internal reality. I say internal because everything we experience in life is internal, even though it might come from an external source. Feelings occur within, revelation and understanding only occur within, as does love and hate, fear and joy.

Does the possibility that Jesus was human affect his teaching? Yes, it makes Jesus' teachings available to those of us who are not Gods and do not understand the ways of Gods. It makes his teachings manageable for us ordinary people who comprise the multitudes.

Does the possibility that Jesus is God affect his teachings? Yes. It makes us supplicants to those who would place themselves between Jesus and us or God, people who have the same faults, and imperfections and ambitions and foolishness that we ordinary people have.

Can Atheist and Secular people be Christians? Certainly, even if one does not believe in the Old Testament God, or in any God or a different God, it does not matter, Jesus'' teachings are of value to all men and women. Indeed these are the people that might most benefit the most from Jesus' words. The phrase "Do unto others as you would have them do unto you" resonates among all people except those who are selfish, greedy, and those who seek power over others.

He said that he came, 'Not to save the righteous, because the righteous have their own salvation, but to save those who are lost'. This is the third most important rule of Jesus' teachings.

The first is to love your God with all your, and all your mind. The second is to love your neighbor as you do yourself. On these two principles hang all the law and the prophets.

However, if a man is not disposed to loving his God, then let him love his fellow man; this will cause his God to come forth from the darkness.

Christian Authority

The teachings of Jesus are available to all, Atheist, Jew, Muslim and Hindu, Buddhist without insult to their primary belief. This is the scope of Jesus' word.

Jesus was not the founder of the religion we call Christianity. Modern Christianity would be a mystery to Jesus. He was not a Christian; he was a Jew. The earliest of his followers were also Jews who followed Jewish traditions. Jesus meant for his message to be presented only to Mosaic Jews. If Judaism had been an inclusive religion instead of an exclusive religion for only Jews and those born of Jewish mothers, there may never have been either Christians or Muslims.

Mohammad, because of his religious awakening, applied to the Jews in Medina and Mecca, to be the leader of the Jews. Of course, the Jews in Mecca and medina did not have the authority or desire to grant Mohammad his wish and they rejected him and he went on to found Islam. The Roman persecuted Christians because they looked to Jerusalem for religious guidance, and would not accept Roman authority. When the Romans faced the fact, that like the Jews, whose state they eventually destroyed, the Christians would not submit to Roman pressure either. Constantine I, being an astute politician, made the Roman Christian Church an offer they could not refuse, a chance to become the state religion.

The official Christian Church, the Roman Catholic Church as we know it today was founded in Nicaea in 325 AD with the explicit approval and authority of Constantine I as Emperor of the

Roman Empire. It was by Constantine's authority that Christianity was officially founded.

One might ask in response to this, "By what authority do 'you' say this?"

I would have to answer, "By the authority given me by Jesus. From the same source that gave Jesus, or Mohammad or the Buddha their authority to speak the words and do the deeds that were part of their destiny,"

This is something that I say reluctantly, because there is no way to prove this. Thus, it would not be wise for anyone to believe me just because I say so or just because anyone says so. It is not necessary to believe or disbelieve everything one hears or sees. I see magicians do tricks but I do not believe them, no matter what I see. It is not necessary for me to believe in electromagnetic radiation in order for radios to work

I do not pretend to know who Jesus was or what he was. I know no more about Jesus than Simon did when he first encountered Jesus while fishing and Jesus said to him, "Follow me, I will make you a fisher of men".

I do not know Gods' thoughts and I do not know Gods plan. If anyone knew Gods' thoughts, they would be like gods themselves.

Therefore, if you do not believe me, then that would not be unreasonable.

I began my religious life and training as a Christian. I went to Sunday school. I was taught the stories from the Old Testament, and on Christmas and Easter, I was taught about Jesus' birth, death, and his life.

At the age of 13 or so, I lost interest. I just did not believe the ridiculous stories from the Old Testament, about the creation of the world and the stories about Adam and Eve and the snake and the apple as the reason for the human condition. I became what I thought was an atheist. Even though not believing in the Old Testament God is not atheism.

At about the age of 16 or 17 I noticed that my father never went to church and never talked about religion. One day I asked him what he believed in. He told me that he believed in the teachings of Jesus as reported in the New Testament of the Bible, and not the rest of the Bible. I do not know where he got his view, I did not think to ask, but I was satisfied with his answer. Even though my father lived to be 101, I never talked about religion with him again.

My next experience with these issues came when I was about 20. I had a near death experience. I was choking on a foreign object that was caught in my throat. I could not dislodge the object and I felt myself losing consciousness and dying. Just as I was about to black out, a voice came to me from within, it said, with profound calmness, "Do not fear, for I will be with you till the end of time". My fear left me and I prepared to die with the same calmness. Then another voice came from within me and told me what to do to eject the foreign object from my throat. I did what I was instructed to do, with vigor, and the object shot out of my mouth. When I looked up I was on the ground and a group of people were standing over me. I composed myself and I told them that I was all right and I got up and left.

The memories of that voice and the words about not being afraid have always been with me since then. While I did not stop being an atheist from an Old Testament point of view, I knew that I was not atheist in general.

I tell about that even because it gave me perspective when the Christ came to me.

I was walking beside an expressway by myself on an afternoon summer day. I was about 26 or 27. I remember that I was reflecting on how the flow of traffic looked like a river. Suddenly I had the feeling and experience that I had become transformed into Jesus. Even so, at the same time I was absolutely clear that I was still me. I understood Jesus' teachings. I realized that I was not an atheist. I realized that I had been looking in the wrong place. Like the voice that I heard earlier in my near death experience, this experience was something that came from within me and not without. I understood what Jesus meant when he said that 'God is in the kingdom of heaven and the kingdom of heaven is within you.'

It should be pointed out that this type of epiphany or revelation of visionary event is the basis for all religion. No one was with Jesus, Mohammad, or Moses when they went up on their respective mountains. No one was with the Buddha when he sat under the Boddhi tree and achieved his enlightenment to the Law, or what the Hindu Bodhisattvas saw upon their enlightenment. Constantine I saw a vision in the sky of a cross, emblazoned with the words, "By this will you conquer", but he was the only one who saw it. When he saw it, he made a promise that he would convert to Christianity, and convert Christianity to Roman authority. Without prophets and seers, there would be no religion.

Before I write about details of what was revealed to me in my transformation, it is necessary to explain why religion, in general, is so popular and has such a profound effect on so many people, even those who have not had revelations themselves and those who do not believe.

Religions offer us the pleasure that comes from our belief, their familiarity, the sense of knowing the truth, and the sense of belonging and sharing a common faith. Religion also offers us a coping mechanism for dealing with the negative, unpredictable, fearful, uncertain and relative nature of the physical world.

Islam and Judaism, which are much closer to each other than they are to Christianity, use a system of laws and rules handed down by God, which, if followed, can mitigate the effects and fears we have about death, life after death, the uncertainty of life and the possibility of suffering in hell after life is over.

Although there are those who say that Jesus chose to die for our sins, this is not true. He did not choose his destiny; he acted it out. He did not control Judas, the Sanhedrin, Pontius Pilate, Herod, or the Roman desire to kill someone at that time. He did not control John the Baptist. To chose to die is to commit suicide and is a cowards' way out. To accept a death that is our destiny, to save others, is a thing of wonder. Like a man, Jesus weakened before his death. He asked God to remove the cup of death from him, but it did not happen, that was his destiny. Jesus had no choice except to do God's will, which is exactly what he did.

How is it possible that God does not know the time and method of the death of each one of us? How is it possible that God does not know the future of each one of us? How is it possible that we or any human could do something that was not an expression of God's will? There are those who say that God is flawed in his knowledge. That God does not want to know what people will do, for entertainment purposes, so he can see the outcome. So he can get mad when people do not act according to his rules, and then punish them with sadistic glee, when they express the imperfections he created them with.

There are those who say that God created us in his own image. If God is like us and created us in his image, then that God is a damn fool. Any God who created Hitler in his image is a maniac.

Arian Christianity as drawn from the words of Jesus of Nazareth offers a different approach. Jesus knew months before he came to Jerusalem that he would be crucified and killed. This was his destiny. This was the destiny he was born to. Deep down, we all know what destiny is; it is what actually happens. We do not have to guess what destiny is, it is what happens. It is the ultimate expression of God's will. There are no other options than what God has willed. Even unbelievers know that 'this' moment is dependent on the moment that preceded it, and that moment was dependent on the moment that preceded that, and these moments are consistent from beginning to end.

How could it be that Jesus the Christ, the Son of God, the Messiah, even God himself in the Trinitarian view, have a destiny and we ordinary humans do not? How is it that Jesus says, "Even the hairs of your head ore numbered." and the days of our lives are not? Death will take us all in its own way and in its own time. In the face of this, Jesus tells us, "Do not be afraid, I will be with you until the end of time".

He meant this literally, and not figuratively. Ask yourself, and ask the question, what is the name of the force or process that creates the future and destroys the past? If there is no God, this must happen through a physical force that has some name or identity. If God does it, then the whole of time is within his knowledge and there is nothing that can happen without his knowledge. Even if God does it, it must be done by the action of some physical force that can be named.

I submit to you that there is no such power. Jesus still walks beside the Sea of Galilee. He has always walked there. He is still there on the cross, dying for us. Just as he has always been there, we have always been here since the beginning of time. Because we can see only 'this' moment, we are blind to **the sweep of God's Time, which is eternal and whole and consistent from beginning to end.**

If God is subject to time as we are, then there is a principle or power that is greater than God. If God is the creator of time then there is no need for there to be a force that creates the future and destroys the past moment by moment.

We have always been here. God is aware of the totality of time and not just the moment. This is the majesty of his creation, profound beyond words or scripture, incalculable in its scope.

Where is this God? Exactly where Jesus says he is, in the kingdom of heaven, which is within us.

When we see and hear things, we see and hear light and sound waves that are projected from objects to our eyes and ears and then processed by our organs of perception and cognition and then projected back out onto the world as sight and sound. What we see and hear happens within. When we win or lose, when experience pleasure or when we suffer, it takes place inside us and not outside. Then why should it be strange that God can be found within us where we live and experience life?

The reach of Jesus' teachings extends beyond words, scripture, and science. Our connection to those parts of us that live in different times is within also. The destiny that we experience is the same as the destiny that Jesus experienced, except we are not Jesus. If Jesus were human he would know what we feel, if he were not then he would know nothing about us.

Children of 3 or 4 years are killed by sickness, murder or war. What just God would do this to the innocent? He does not; these children are still alive. Each person, each thing, each thought, is an integral part of the perfect world that God created, where the imperfections are the result of our ignorance and our desires for the world to be something other than what it is.

The Pillars of the Heart

The apostle Paul said that the source of faith was hearing the word, (or reading it). For Arian Christians the 'word', is not the scripture of the Old Testament, but the words of Jesus as reported in the New Testament in the Gospels of Matthew, Mark, Luke and John, and for Arian Christians, the Arian Christian Bible, which consists of the books of Matthew, Mark and Luke in any Holy Bible. This is the first pillar of the heart.

The second pillar is, "Do unto others as you would have them do unto you"

The third is, "Love your God with all your heart, soul and mind".

The way we establish these pillars is by reading the Gospels of the Apostles Matthew, mark and Luke.

APPENDIX

The appended material and discussions were adapted from Wikipedia and other public domain sources, and is provided as reference material only.

The Messiah

Messiah is a term used by Jews, Christians, and Muslims for the redeemer figure expected in one form or another by each religion.

The word originally came from Hebrew messiah, "anointed". In Judaism, the expected king of the Davidic line who would deliver Israel from foreign bondage and restore the glories of its golden age. The Greek New Testament's translation of the term, Christos, became the accepted Christian designation and title of Jesus of Nazareth, indicative of the principal character and function of his ministry. More loosely, the term messiah denotes any redeemer figure; and the adjective messianic is used in a broad sense to refer to beliefs or theories about an eschatological improvement of the state of humanity or the world.[1]

In Jewish messianic tradition and eschatology, *messiah* refers to a leader anointed by God, and in some cases, a future King of Israel, physically descended from the Davidic line, who will rule the people of a united tribes of Israel[2] and herald the Messianic Age[3] of global peace. In Judaism, the Messiah is not considered to be the literal, physical God or Son of God.

Christians believe that prophecies in the Hebrew Bible refer to a spiritual savior, partly evidenced in selectively culled passages from the Book of Isaiah: "Therefore the Lord himself will give you a sign: The young woman is with child, and will give birth to a son, and will call him Immanuel,"[Isa. 7:14] and, in a different chapter, "He was pierced for our transgressions, he was crushed for our iniquities; the punishment that brought us peace was upon him, and by his wounds we are healed,"[Isa. 53:5] and believe Jesus of Nazareth to be that Messiah (Christ).

Etymology

The (Greek) Septuagint version of the Old Testament renders all thirty-nine instances of the Hebrew word for *anointed* (*Mašíaḥ*) as *Khristós*

(Χριστός).[4] The New Testament records the Greek transliteration Μεσσίας, *Messias* twice in John.[Jn. 1:41][4:25]**Messiah** (Hebrew: מָשִׁיחַ, Modern *Mashiah* Tiberian *Māšîăḥ*; in modern Jewish texts in English sometimes spelled *Moshiach*; Aramaic: משיחא, Greek: Μεσσίας, Syriac: ܡܫܝܚܐ, *Məšîḥā*, Arabic: المسيح, *al-Masīḥ*, Latin: *Messias*) literally means "anointed (one)". In standard Hebrew, The Messiah is often referred to as מֶלֶךְ הַמָּשִׁיחַ, Méleḫ ha-Mašíaḥ (in the Tiberian vocalization pronounced Mélek haMMāšîªḥ), literally meaning "the Anointed King." In Islam, Isa (Jesus) is also called the Messiah (*Masih*),[5] who will come back to earth a second time before the last day.

Judaism

Belief in the eventual coming of a future, great messiah, The Messiah *(Moshiach)*, is said to be a basic and fundamental part of traditional Judaism, though not all in the religion agree.[6] Modern scholars point out that the idea of *The* Messiah is not mentioned anywhere in the Torah (the first five books of the Bible). They point out that the grand messianic concept was introduced during the age of the prophets (which was later in the history of Judaism). Traditional Judaism disagrees with these scholars, maintaining instead that idea of *The* Messiah has always been a part of Judaism.

The concept of the coming of The Messiah was held in the highest regard by pre-Christian Judaism. The Talmud records: "All the prophets prophesied [all the good things] only in respect of the Messianic era."[7] In another folio, the Talmud says, "The Jews are destined to eat [their fill] in the days of the Messiah," and "The world was created only...for the sake of the Messiah."[8]

A prominent Judaism Web site claims:

Belief in the eventual coming of the *moshiach*...is part of the minimum requirements of Jewish belief. In the Shemoneh Esrei prayer, recited three times daily, we pray for all of the elements of the coming of the moshiach: gathering of the exiles; restoration of the religious courts of justice; an end of wickedness, sin, and heresy; reward to the righteous; rebuilding of Jerusalem; restoration of the line of King David; and restoration of Temple service.[6]

The literal translation of the word, messiah (moshiach), is "anointed," which refers to a ritual of consecrating someone or something by putting holy oil upon it.[1 Sam. 10:1-2] It is used throughout the Jewish Bible in reference to a wide variety of individuals and objects; for example, a Jewish king,[1 Kings 1:39] Jewish priests,[Lev. 4:3] and prophets,[Isa. 61:1] the Jewish Temple and its utensils,[Ex. 40:9-11] unleavened bread,[Num. 6:15] and a non-Jewish king (Cyrus king of Persia).[Isa. 45:1]

A common modern **rabbinic** interpretation is that there is a *potential* messiah in every generation. The Talmud, which often uses stories to make a moral point (*aggadah*), tells of a highly respected **rabbi** who found the Messiah at the gates of **Rome** and asked him, "When will you finally come?" He was quite surprised when he was told, "Today." Overjoyed and full of anticipation, the man waited all day. The next day he returned, disappointed and puzzled, and asked, "You said messiah would come 'today' but he didn't come! What happened?" The Messiah replied, "Scripture says, 'Today, 'if you will but hearken to His voice.'"[Ps. 95:7]

Judaism believes in a unique future physical messiah who will usher in the messianic age of peace to the world.

In Judaism today, as always, the fervent - in the words of Rambam - "believe in the coming of the Messiah and await it daily although it may be delayed." As religious Jews were herded into the gas chambers by the Nazis, a song arose as if to proclaim that no force can wreck their trust in the Messianic future, to the words of the Rambam.

Particularly the Chabad movement - the largest and most influential Jewish outreach movement today [promoting Judaism and morality to Jews and gentiles] has a fervent hope that the Messianic age is manifesting through the radical positive changes occurring, for example the miraculous turnaround in Russian policy to free her Jews. Whereas such cataclysmic regime changes necessitated bloodshed [of epic proportions] in the past, miraculously Michael Gorbachav of his own accord freed the Jews whom were subject to the harshest of torment, exile, and imprisonment for over seventy years. Furthermore as if to underscore the Messianic notion in play, hundreds of thousands of these Jews emigrated to Israel - fulfilling the Biblical Prophecy "even if you will be in the farthest places of earth I will return you (to Israel").

To the Jew, the Messiah has a most important mission, namely to bring the world back to G-d, and make it a place of peace, justice and harmony. When Jesus failed to accomplish this, the early Christians had to radically alter the very concept of the Messiah. This, in turn, transformed Christianity from another Jewish Messianic sect into a religion that is quite alien to many basic Jewish teachings.[9]

Christianity

Christianity emerged early in the first century A.D. as a movement among Jews and their Gentile converts who believed that Jesus was the Messiah. The name of "Christian" refers to the Greek word for 'Messiah': *Khristos* (χριστος). Christians commonly refer to Jesus as either the "Christ" or the "Messiah." In Christian theology the two words are synonymous.

Christians believe Jesus to be the Messiah that Jews were expecting:

The first thing Andrew did was to find his brother Simon and tell him, "We have found the Messiah" (that is, the Christ). And he brought him to Jesus.[Jn. 1:41-42]

The Christian concept of the Christ/Messiah as "the Word made Flesh" (see also Logos) is fundamentally different from the Jewish and Islamic in that the majority of historical and mainline Christian theologies, as seen within the Nicene Creed, consider Jesus to be God or God the Son.

Christians believe that Daniel (Hebrew: דָּנִיֵּאל, or Daniyyel) was a prophet and gave an indication of when the Messiah, the prince *mashiyach nagiyd*, would come.[Dan. 9:25-26] Daniel's prophecies refer to him as a descendant of King David, a Son of Man, who will rebuild the nation of Israel, destroy the wicked, and ultimately judge the whole world.

In Christian theology, the Christ/Messiah serves five main functions:[10]

- He suffers and dies to make atonement before God for the sins of all humanity, because His justice requires that sins be punished, according to Penal substitution theology.[11]
- He was raised from the dead on the third day after He was crucified to prove that He has defeated death and the power of Satan, thus enabling those that receive Him as their Savior to live under God's grace rather than the strict laws of Judaism [Galatians 2:16]

- He serves as the pioneer, embodiment of the culture and living presence of the kingdom of God
- He will establish peace and rule the world during the Millennial Kingdom, which will immediately follow the tribulation. See Nicene Creeds of 325 and 381 A.D.:

"And I saw thrones, and they sat upon them, and judgment was given unto them: and I saw the souls of them that were beheaded for the witness of Jesus, and for the word of God, and which had not worshipped the beast, neither his image, neither had received his mark upon their foreheads, or in their hands; and they lived and reigned with Christ a thousand years. But the rest of the dead lived not again until the thousand years were finished. This is the first resurrection. Blessed and holy is he that hath part in the first resurrection: on such the second death hath no power, but they shall be priests of God and of Christ, and shall reign with him a thousand years."

- He is the God of Abraham, Isaac and Jacob and he came to earth as a human. John 1:1-2,14a: *In the beginning was the*

66

Word and the Word was with God and the Word was God. He was in the beginning with God. 14a And the Word became flesh and dwelt among us. John 8:58: *Most assuredly, I say to you, before Abraham was, I AM.*

In the New Testament, Jesus often referred to himself as 'Son of Man'which Christianity interprets as a reference to Daniel 7:13-14 (KJV):

"I saw in the night visions, and, behold, one like the Son of man came with the clouds of heaven, and came to the Ancient of days, and they brought him near before him. And there was given him dominion, and glory, and a kingdom, that all people, nations, and languages, should serve him: his dominion is an everlasting dominion, which shall not pass away, and his kingdom that which shall not be destroyed."[Daniel 7:7,13]

Because Christians believe that Jesus is the Messiah, and that he claimed to be the Son of Man referred to by Daniel, Christianity interprets Daniel 7:13-14 as a statement of the Messiah's authority and that the Messiah will have an everlasting kingdom. Jesus' use of this title is seen as a direct claim to be the Messiah. Some identified Jesus as the Messiah,[Mk. 8:29] his opponents accused him of such a claim,[Lk. 23:2] and he is recorded at least twice as asserting it himself directly.[Mk. 14:60-62] [Jn. 4:25-26]

Christianity interprets a wide range of biblical passages in the Old Testament (Hebrew scripture) as predicting the coming of the Messiah and believes that they are following Jesus' own explicit teaching:

- He said to them..."Then he said unto them, O fools, and slow of heart to believe all that the prophets have spoken: Ought not Christ to have suffered these things, and to enter into his glory? And beginning at Moses and all the prophets, he expounded unto them in all the scriptures the things concerning himself."[Lk. 24:25-27]
- "Then opened he their understanding, that they might understand the scriptures, And said unto them, Thus it is

written, and thus it behooved Christ to suffer, and to rise from the dead the third day: And that repentance and remission of sins should be preached in his name among all nations, beginning at Jerusalem."[Lk. 24:45-47]

- The book of Matthew repeatedly says, "This was to fulfill the prophecy...."

Christianity believes all of the Messianic prophecies concerning His first coming to earth were fulfilled in the mission, death, and resurrection of Jesus, and seeks to spread throughout the world its interpretation that the Messiah is the only Saviour, and that Jesus will return to fulfill the rest of Messianic prophecy in human form.

Islam

The Qur'an states Jesus is the Messiah,[Qur'an 3:45] and Muslims believe Jesus is alive in Heaven and will return to Earth to defeat the Dajjal, or Antichrist. A hadith in Abu Dawud (Sunnan Abu Dawud 37:4310) states:

Narrated Abu Hurayrah: The Prophet said: There is no prophet between me and him, that is, Jesus. He will descend (to the earth). When you see him, recognise him: a man of medium height, reddish hair, wearing two light yellow garments, looking as if drops were falling down from his head though it will not be wet. He will fight for the cause of Islam. He will break the cross, kill the swine, and put an end to war (in another Tradition, there is the word Jizyah instead of *Harb* (war), meaning that he will abolish jizyah); God will perish all religions except Islam. He will destroy the Antichrist and will live on the earth for forty and then he will die. The Muslims will pray behind him.

Shia Muslims believe al-Mahdi will arrive first, and after him, Jesus. Jesus will proclaim that the true leader is al-Mahdi. A war, literally Jihad (Jihade Asghar) will be fought - the Dajjal (evil) against al-Mahdi and Jesus (good). This war will mark the approach of the coming of the

Last Day. After Jesus slays al-Dajjāl at the Gate of <u>Lud</u>, Muslims believe he will marry and have children. During his life, he will have revealed that <u>Islam</u> is the last word of God.shia concept about Mehdi is full of controversy as they believe of Mehdi match those of jews. A <u>hadith</u> in <u>Sahih Bukhari</u> (<u>4:55:658</u>) says:

> Allah's Apostle said "How will you be when the son of Mary descends amongst you and your Imam is from amongst you."

Very few scholars outside of Orthodox Islam reject all the quotes (Hadith) attributed to Muhammad that mention the second return of Jesus, the Dajjal and <u>Imam Mahdi</u>, believing that they have no Qur'anic basis. However, the vast majority of Muslim scholars disagree with the implication of termination of Jesus' life when he was allegedly crucified (for example Yusuf Ali's translation reads: "O Jesus! I will take thee and raise thee to Myself"). Verses ^[<u>Qur'an 4:157</u>] imply that Jesus was not killed physically but it appeared as such in some other sense; Verse ^[<u>Qur'an 19:33</u>] implies that Jesus will die someday. The vast majority of Muslims, and the unified opinion of Islam maintain that the bodily death of Jesus will happen after his second coming. Many classical commentators such as Ibn Kathir, At-Tabari, al-Qurtubi, Suyuti, al-Undlusi (Bahr al-Muhit), Abu al-Fadl al-Alusi (Ruh al-Maani) clearly mention that verse ^[<u>Qur'an 43:61</u>] of the Qur'an refers to the descent of Jesus before the Day of Resurrection, indicating that Jesus would be the Sign that the Hour is close.

> And (Jesus) shall be a Sign (for the coming of) the Hour (of Judgment): therefore have no doubt about the (Hour)...
> [<u>Qur'an 43:61</u>]

Those that reject the second coming of Jesus argue that the knowledge of the Hour is only with God, and that the Hour will come suddenly. They maintain that if the second coming of Jesus were true, whenever it happens, billions of people would then be certain the Hour is about to come. The response given to this is that signs that the Last Hour is near have been foretold and given, including that of the second coming of Jesus, as signs indicating the Last Hour is near. They will not clarify when it is to come in any specific sense, and hence do not reveal it. Christianity avoids this conflict because Jesus is part of the Trinity of

God (Father, Son (Jesus), Holy Spirit), and the second coming of Jesus signifies the beginning of the period of Tribulation.

Allama Iqbal while commenting on the second coming of Jesus said, "It is the basic idea of Magian religion, for it contains implicitly the conception of the world-historical struggle between Good and Evil, with the power of Evil prevailing in the middle period, and the Good finally triumphant on the Day of Judgement. If this view of the prophetic teaching is meant to apply to Islam it is obviously a misrepresentation. The point to note is that the Magian admitted the existence of false gods; only they did not turn to worship them. Islam denies the very existence of false gods."

Islam Ahmadiyya

In Ahmadiyya Islam, the terms "Messiah" and "Mahdi" (Messiah of Islam) are synonymous terms for one and the same person. Like the term Messiah which, among other meanings, in essence means being *anointed* by God or *appointed* by God the term "Mahdi" means *guided* by God, thus both imply a direct ordainment and a spiritual nurturing by God of a divinely chosen individual.[citation needed] According to Ahmadiyya thought, Messiahship is a phenomenon, through which a special emphasis is given on the transformation of a people by way of offering suffering for the sake of God instead of giving suffering (i.e. refraining from revenge). Ahmadis believe that this special emphasis was given through the person of Jesus and Mirza Ghulam Ahmad [15] among others.

Ahmadis hold that the prophesied eschatological figures of various religions, the coming of the Messiah and Mahdi in fact were to be fulfilled in one person who was to represent all previous prophets. The prophecies concerning the Mahdi or the second coming of Jesus are seen by Ahmadis as metaphorical, in that one was to be born and rise within the dispensation of Muhammad, who by virtue of his similarity and affinity with Jesus of Nazareth, and the similarity in nature, temperament and disposition of the people of Jesus' time and the people of the time of the promised one (the Mahdi) is called by the same name.

Numerous Hadith are presented by the Ahmadis in support of their view such as one from Sunan Ibn Majah which says:

"   *There is No Mahdi but Jesus son of Mary*   "

—Ibn Majah, Bab, Shahadatu-Zaman

Ahmadis believe that the prophecies concerning the Mahdi and the second coming of Jesus have been fulfilled in the person of Mirza Ghulam Ahmad of Qadian (1835–1908) the founder of the Ahmadiyya Movement. Contrary to mainstream Islam the Ahmadis do not believe that Jesus is alive in heaven, but that he survived the crucifixion and migrated towards the east where he died a natural death and that Ghulam Ahmad was only the promised spiritual second coming and likeness of Jesus, the promised Messiah and Mahdi.

Other traditions

- Bahá'u'lláh, founder of the Bahá'í Faith, claimed to be the figure prophesied in the scriptures of the world's religions.

- Adherents to the Unification Movement consider Rev. Dr. Sun Myung Moon to be the Second Coming of Jesus Christ figuratively, not literally. They believe he has the mission of Christ (whom they believe isn't God).

- The Shakers believed that Jesus was the male Messiah and Mother Ann Lee, the female Messiah.

- For the Rastafari movement, Haile Selassie of Ethiopia is the messiah.

Arianism

Arianism is the theological teaching of Arius (<u>ca.</u> AD 250–336), a Christian <u>presbyter</u> from <u>Alexandria</u>, Egypt, concerning the relationship of the entities of the <u>Trinity</u> ('God the Father', 'God the Son' and 'God the Holy Spirit') and the precise nature of the <u>Son of God</u>. Deemed a <u>heretic</u> by the <u>First Council of Nicaea</u> of 325, Arius was later exonerated in 335 at the <u>First Synod of Tyre</u>[1], and then pronounced a heretic again after his death at the <u>First Council of Constantinople</u> of 381.[2] The Roman Emperors <u>Constantius II</u> (337–361) and <u>Valens</u> (364–378) were Arians or <u>Semi-Arians</u>. The Arian <u>concept of Christ</u> is that the Son of God did not always exist, but was created by—and is therefore distinct from and inferior to—God the Father.[3]

Arianism is defined as those teachings attributed to Arius which are in opposition to mainstream Trinitarian Christological dogma, as determined by the first two <u>Ecumenical Councils</u> and currently maintained by the <u>Roman Catholic Church</u>, the <u>Eastern Orthodox Churches</u> and most <u>Protestant</u> Churches. "Arianism" is also often used to refer to other <u>nontrinitarian</u> theological systems of the 4th century, which regarded <u>Jesus Christ</u>—the Son of God, the <u>Logos</u>—as either a created being (as in Arianism proper and <u>Anomoeanism</u>), or as neither uncreated nor created in the sense other beings are created (as in <u>Semi-Arianism</u>).

Origin of Arian doctrines

Arius taught that God the Father and <u>the Son</u> did not exist together eternally. He taught that the <u>pre-incarnate</u> Jesus was a divine being created by (and therefore inferior to) God the Father at some point, before which the Son did not exist.[4] In English-language works, it is sometimes said that Arians believe that Jesus is or was a "creature"; in the sense of "created being". Arius and his followers appealed to Bible verses such as John 14:28 where Jesus says that the father is "greater than I", and to Proverbs 8:22 which states "The Lord created me at the beginning of his work"[5] although this verse is now generally held to refer to some concept of "wisdom" rather than to the Son of God.[6]

Of all the various disagreements within the Christian Church, the Arian controversy has held the greatest force and power of theological and political conflict, with the possible exception of the Protestant Reformation. The conflict between Arianism and Trinitarian beliefs was the first major doctrinal confrontation in the Church after the legalization of Christianity by the Roman Emperor Constantine I.[citation needed]

The controversy over Arianism began to rise in the late 3rd century and extended over the greater part of the 4th century and involved most church members, simple believers, priests and monks as well as bishops, emperors and members of Rome's imperial family. Yet, such a deep controversy within the Church could not have materialized in the 3rd and 4th centuries without some significant historical influences providing the basis for the Arian doctrines. Most orthodox or mainstream Christian historians define and minimize the Arian conflict as the exclusive construct of Arius and a handful of rogue bishops engaging in heresy. Of the roughly three hundred bishops in attendance at the Council of Nicea, only three bishops did not sign the Nicene Creed. However, to minimize the extent of Arianism ignores the fact that extremely prominent Emperors such as Constantius II, and Valens were Arians, as well as prominent Gothic, Vandal and Lombard warlords both before and after the fall of the Western Roman Empire, and that none of these groups was out of the mainstream of the Roman Empire in the 4th century.[citation needed]

After the dispute over Arius politicized the debate and a catholic or general solution to the debate was sought, with a great majority holding to the Trinitarian position, the Arian position was declared officially to be heterodox. Lucian of Antioch had contended for a christology very similar to what would later be known as Arianism and is thought to have contributed much to its development. Arius was a student of Lucian's private academy in Antioch.

73

While Arianism continued to dominate for several decades even within the family of the Emperor, the Imperial nobility, and higher-ranking clergy, in the end it was Trinitarianism which prevailed in the Roman Empire at the end of the 4th century. Arianism, which had been taught by the Arian missionary Ulfilas to the Germanic tribes, was dominant for some centuries among several Germanic tribes in western Europe, especially Goths and Lombards (and significantly for the late Empire, the Vandals), but ceased to be the mainstream belief by the 8th century. Trinitarianism remained the dominant doctrine in all major branches of the Eastern and Western Church and later within Protestantism.

Beliefs

Because most extant written material on Arianism was written by its opponents, the nature of Arian teachings is difficult to define precisely today. The letter of Auxentius,[7] a 4th-century Arian bishop of Milan, regarding the missionary Ulfilas, gives the clearest picture of Arian beliefs on the nature of the Trinity: God the Father ("unbegotten"), always existing, was separate from the lesser Jesus Christ ("only-begotten"), born before time began and creator of the world. The Father, working through the Son, created the Holy Spirit, who was subservient to the Son as the Son was to the Father. The Father was seen as "the only true God". 1 Corinthians 8:5-6 was cited as proof text:

Indeed, even though there may be so-called gods in heaven or on earth — as in fact there are many gods and many lords — yet for us there is one God (Gk. *theos* - θεος), the Father, from whom are all things and for whom we exist, and one Lord (*kyrios* - κυριος), Jesus Christ, through whom are all things and through whom we exist.
—NRSV

A letter from Arius to the Arian Eusebius of Nicomedia succinctly states the core beliefs of the Arians:

Some of them say that the Son is an eructation, others that he is a production, others that he is also unbegotten. These are impieties to which we cannot listen, even though the heretics threaten us with a thousand deaths. But we say and believe and have taught, and do teach, that the Son is not unbegotten, nor in any way part of the unbegotten; and that he does not derive his subsistence from any matter; but that by his own will and counsel he has subsisted before time and before ages as perfect God, only begotten and unchangeable, and that before he was begotten, or created, or purposed, or established, he was not. For he was not unbegotten. We are persecuted, because we say that the Son has a beginning, but that God is without beginning.

—Peters, *Heresy and Authority in Medieval Europe*, p. 41

First Council of Nicaea and its aftermath

A 4th-century miniature of the Council of Nicaea, which condemned Arius's teaching

In 321, Arius was denounced by a synod at Alexandria for teaching a heterodox view of the relationship of Jesus to God the Father. Because Arius and his followers had great influence in the schools of Alexandria—counterparts to modern universities or seminaries—their theological views spread, especially in the eastern Mediterranean.

By 325, the controversy had become significant enough that the Emperor Constantine called an assembly of bishops, the First Council of Nicaea, which condemned Arius' doctrine and formulated the Original Nicene Creed[8], forms of which are still recited in Catholic, Orthodox, Anglican, and some Protestant services. The Nicene Creed's central term, used to describe the relationship between the Father and the Son, is Homoousios, or Consubstantiality, meaning "of the same substance" or "of one being". (The Athanasian Creed is less often used but is a more overtly anti-Arian statement on the Trinity.)

The focus of the Council of Nicaea was the divinity of Christ (see Paul of Samosata and the Synods of Antioch). Arius taught that Jesus Christ was divine and was sent to earth for the salvation of mankind but that Jesus Christ was not equal to the Father (infinite, primordial origin) and to the Holy Spirit (giver of life). Under Arianism, Christ was instead not consubstantial with God the Father [9] since both the Father and the Son under Arius were made of "like" essence or being (see homoiousia) but not of the same essence or being (see homoousia).[9] Ousia is essence or being, in Eastern Christianity, and is the aspect of God that is completely incomprehensible to mankind and human perception. It is all that subsists by itself and which has not its being in another.[10] God the Father and God the Son and God the Holy Spirit all being uncreated.[11] According to the teaching of Arius, the preexistent Logos and thus the incarnate Jesus Christ was a created being; that only the Son was directly created and begotten by God the Father, before ages, but was of a distinct, though similar, essence or substance to the Creator; his opponents argued that this would make Jesus less than God, and that this was heretical.[9] Much of the distinction between the differing factions was over the phrasing that Christ expressed in the New Testament to express submission to God the Father.[9] The theological term for this submission is kenosis. This Ecumenical council declared that Jesus Christ was a distinct being of God in existence or reality (hypostasis), which the Latin fathers translated as persona. Jesus was God in essence, being and or nature (ousia), which the Latin fathers translated as substantia.

Constantine is believed to have exiled those who refused to accept the Nicean creed—Arius himself, the deacon Euzoios, and the Libyan bishops Theonas of Marmarica and Secundus of Ptolemais—and also the bishops who signed the creed but refused to join in condemnation of Arius, Eusebius of Nicomedia and Theognis of Nicaea. The Emperor also ordered all copies of the *Thalia*, the book in which Arius had expressed his teachings, to be burned. However, there is no evidence that his son and ultimate successor, Constantius II, who was an Arian Christian, was exiled.

Although he was committed to maintaining what the church had defined at Nicaea, Constantine was also bent on pacifying the situation and eventually became more lenient toward those condemned and exiled at the council. First he allowed Eusebius of Nicomedia, who was a protégé of his sister, and Theognis to return once they had signed an ambiguous statement of faith. The two, and other friends of Arius, worked for Arius' rehabilitation. At the First Synod of Tyre in AD 335, they brought accusations against Athanasius, bishop of Alexandria, the primary opponent of Arius; after this, Constantine had Athanasius banished, since he considered him an impediment to reconciliation. In the same year, the Synod of Jerusalem under Constantine's direction readmitted Arius to communion in AD 336. Arius, however, died on the way to this event in Constantinople. This was the same day Arius' own bishop prayed that if his heresy was to be propagated, the Lord take him in death that night- or better, Arius. Some scholars also suggest that Arius may have been poisoned by his opponents.[12] Eusebius and Theognis remained in the Emperor's favour, and when Constantine, who had been a catechumen much of his adult life, accepted baptism on his deathbed, it was from Eusebius of Nicomedia.

Theological debates

The Council of Nicaea did not end the controversy, as many bishops of the Eastern provinces disputed the *homoousios*, the central term of the Nicene creed, as it had been used by Paul of Samosata, who had advocated a monarchianist Christology. Both the man and his teaching, including the term *homoousios*, had been condemned by the Synods of Antioch in 269.

Hence, after Constantine's death in 337, open dispute resumed again. Constantine's son Constantius II, who had become Emperor of the eastern part of the Empire, actually encouraged the Arians and set out to reverse the Nicene creed. His advisor in these affairs was Eusebius of Nicomedia, who had already at the Council of Nicea been the head of the Arian party, who also was made bishop of Constantinople.

Constantius used his power to exile bishops adhering to the Nicene creed, especially Athanasius of Alexandria, who fled to Rome. In 355 Constantius became the sole Emperor and extended his pro-Arian policy toward the western provinces, frequently using force to push through his creed, even exiling Pope Liberius and installing Antipope Felix II.

As debates raged in an attempt to come up with a new formula, three camps evolved among the opponents of the Nicene creed. The first group mainly opposed the Nicene terminology and preferred the term *homoiousios* (alike in substance) to the Nicene *homoousios*, while they rejected Arius and his teaching and accepted the equality and coeternality of the persons of the Trinity. Because of this centrist position, and despite their rejection of Arius, they were called "semi-Arians" by their opponents. The second group also avoided invoking the name of Arius, but in large part followed Arius' teachings and, in another attempted compromise wording, described the Son as being like (*homoios*) the Father. A third group explicitly called upon Arius and described the Son as unlike (*anhomoios*) the Father. Constantius wavered in his support between the first and the second party, while harshly persecuting the third.

The debates between these groups resulted in numerous synods, among them the Council of Sardica in 343, the Council of Sirmium in 358 and the double Council of Rimini and Seleucia in 359, and no less than fourteen further creed formulas between 340 and 360, leading the pagan observer Ammianus Marcellinus to comment sarcastically: "The highways were covered with galloping bishops." None of these attempts was acceptable to the defenders of Nicene orthodoxy: writing about the latter councils, Saint Jerome remarked that the world "awoke with a groan to find itself Arian."

After Constantius' death in 361, his successor Julian, a devotee of Rome's pagan gods, declared that he would no longer attempt to favor one church faction over another, and allowed all exiled bishops to return; this had the objective of further increasing dissension among Christians. The Emperor Valens, however, revived Constantius' policy and supported the "Homoian" party, exiling bishops and often using force. During this persecution many bishops were exiled to the other ends of the Empire, (e.g., Hilarius of Poitiers to the Eastern provinces). These contacts and the common plight subsequently led to a rapprochement between the Western supporters of the Nicene creed and the *homoousios* and the Eastern semi-Arians.

Theodosius and the Council of Constantinople

It was not until the co-reigns of Gratian and Theodosius that Arianism was effectively wiped out among the ruling class and elite of the Eastern Empire. Theodosius' wife St Flacilla was instrumental in his campaign to end Arianism. Valens died in the Battle of Adrianople in 378 and was succeeded by Theodosius I, who adhered to the Nicene creed. This allowed for settling the dispute.

Two days after Theodosius arrived in Constantinople, November 24, 380, he expelled the Homoian bishop, Demophilus of Constantinople, and surrendered the churches of that city to Gregory Nazianzus, the leader of the rather small Nicene community there, an act which provoked rioting. Theodosius had just been baptized, by bishop Acholius of Thessalonica, during a severe illness, as was common in the early Christian world. In February he and Gratian published an edict[13] that all their subjects should profess the faith of the bishops of Rome and Alexandria (i.e., the Nicene faith), or be handed over for punishment for not doing so.

Although much of the church hierarchy in the East had opposed the Nicene creed in the decades leading up to Theodosius' accession, he managed to achieve unity on the basis of the Nicene creed. In 381, at the Second Ecumenical Council in Constantinople, a group of mainly Eastern bishops assembled and accepted the Nicene Creed of 381,[14] which was supplemented in regard to the Holy Spirit, as well as some other changes: see Comparison between Creed of 325 and Creed of 381. This is generally considered the end of the dispute about the Trinity and the end of Arianism among the Roman, non-Germanic peoples.

Early medieval Germanic kingdoms

However, during the time of Arianism's flowering in Constantinople, the Gothic convert Ulfilas (later the subject of the letter of Auxentius cited above) was sent as a missionary to the Gothic barbarians across the Danube, a mission favored for political reasons by emperor Constantius II. Ulfilas' initial success in converting this Germanic people to an Arian form of Christianity was strengthened by later events. When the Germanic peoples entered the Roman Empire and founded successor-kingdoms in the western part, most had been Arian Christians for more than a century.[citation needed]

The conflict in the 4th century had seen Arian and Nicene factions struggling for control of the Church. In contrast, in the Arian German kingdoms established on the wreckage of the Western Roman Empire in the 5th century, there were entirely separate Arian and Nicene Churches with parallel hierarchies, each serving different sets of believers. The Germanic elites were Arians, and the majority population was Nicene.[citation needed] Many scholars see the persistence of Germanic Arianism as a strategy that was followed in order to differentiate the Germanic elite from the local inhabitants and their culture and also to maintain the Germanic elite's separate group identity.[citation needed]

Most Germanic tribes were generally tolerant of the Nicene beliefs of their subjects. However, the Vandals tried for several decades to force their Arian beliefs on their North African Nicene subjects, exiling Nicene clergy, dissolving monasteries, and exercising heavy pressure on non-conforming Christians.

By the beginning of the 8th century, these kingdoms had either been conquered by Nicene neighbors (Ostrogoths, Vandals, Burgundians) or their rulers had accepted Nicene Christianity (Visigoths, Lombards).

The Franks were unique among the Germanic peoples in that they entered the empire as pagans and converted to Nicene(Catholic) Christianity directly, guided by their king Clovis.[15]

Remnants in the West

However, much of southeastern Europe and central Europe, including many of the Goths and Vandals respectively, had embraced Arianism (the Visigoths converted to Arian Christianity in 376), which led to Arianism being a religious factor in various wars in the Roman Empire.[16] In the west, organized Arianism survived in North Africa, in Hispania, and parts of Italy until it was finally suppressed in the 6th and 7th centuries (in part due to the advance of Islam). Later, during the Protestant reformation, a religious sect in Poland known as the Polish Brethren were commonly referred to as Arians due to their rejection of the Trinity.

"Arian" as a religious insult

In many ways, the conflict around Arian beliefs in the fourth, fifth and sixth centuries helped firmly define the centrality of the Trinity in Nicene Christian theology. As the first major intra-Christian conflict after Christianity's legalization, the struggle between Nicenes and Arians left a deep impression on the institutional memory of Nicene churches.

Archbishop Dmitri of the Orthodox Church in America said Islam is the largest descendant of Arianism today. There is some superficial similarity in Islam's teaching that Jesus was a great prophet, but very distinct from God, although Islam sees Jesus as a human messenger of God without the divine properties that Arianism attributes to Christ. Islam sees itself as a continuation of the Jewish and Christian traditions and reveres many of the same prophets, though Islam denies the crucifixion and resurrection of Jesus and historical Arians claimed it.

Thus, over the past 1,500 years, some Christians have used the term *Arian* to refer to those groups that see themselves as worshiping Jesus Christ or respecting his teachings, but do not hold to the Nicene creed. Despite the frequency with which this name is used as a polemical label, there has been no historically continuous survival of Arianism into the modern era.

Other religious movements considered Arian

There have been religious movements holding beliefs that either they, or their opponents, have considered Arian. To quote the *Encyclopædia Britannica's* article on Arianism: "In modern times some Unitarians are virtually Arians in that they are unwilling either to reduce Christ to a mere human being or to attribute to him a divine nature identical with that of the Father."[17] However, their doctrines cannot be considered representative of traditional Arian doctrines or vice-versa.

A religious movement reputed to practice a form of Arianism (or "Semi-Arianism") are Jehovah's Witnesses.[18] They consider Jesus Christ to be divine and unlike other creatures, but not equal to the one God. And although they are not Trinitarians or Athanasians, they disagree with Arius' views in many respects. Arius, for example, denied that the Son could really know the Father while Jehovah's Witnesses believe that the Son 'fully knows' the Father, and also that the Son, as 'the Word who became flesh', is "the one that has explained him." (Mt 11:27; Joh 1:14, 18) They believe it is vital to come to know God. And although Arius did not accept Athanasius' theory that the Holy Spirit was co-equal and of the same substance as the Father, he did consider the spirit to be a person or a high angel. Jehovah's Witnesses believe the Holy Spirit is not an actual person but rather is God's divine breath or active force.[19]

Historians report that Constantine, who had never been baptized as a Christian during his lifetime, was baptized on his deathbed by the Arian bishop, Eusebius of Nicodemia.[29]

Constantius II, who succeeded Constantine, was an Arian sympathizer[30] who openly encouraged the Arians by appointing Eusebius of Nicomedia, another sympathizer to Arianism, as Bishop ("Patriarch", in the Eastern Church) of Constantinople. Constantius exiled pro-Nicean prelates, including even Pope Liberius. Divisions appeared within the Arian camp, as Semi-Arians attempted to find a compromise between Arianism and Nicene Trinitarianism. A number of synods were held, and at least fourteen different credal formulations were tried throughout the following years, but none proved successful in resolving the dispute.[31] Athanasius continued his vehement opposition to Arianism, soon to be joined by a trio known to history as the Cappadocian Fathers: SS Basil the Great, Gregory the Theologian and Gregory of Nyssa. These four men articulated a theological alternative to Arianism that came to be accepted as the definitive orthodox dogma on the subject.

Following the abortive effort by Julian the Apostate to restore paganism in the empire, the emperor Valens—himself an Arian— renewed the persecution of Nicene hierarchs. However, Valen's successor Theodosius I effectively wiped out Arianism once and for all among the elites of the Eastern Empire through a combination of imperial decree, persecution, and the calling of the Second Ecumenical Council in 381, which condemned Arius anew while reaffirming and expanding the Nicene Creed.[32] This generally ended the influence of Arianism among the non-Germanic peoples of the Roman Empire.

Arianism in the West

Things went differently in the Western Empire. During the reign of Constantius II, the Arian Gothic convert Ulfilas was consecrated a bishop by Eusebius of Nicomedia and sent to missionize his people. His success ensured the survival of Arianism among the Goths and Vandals until the beginning of the eighth century, when these kingdoms succumbed to their Nicean neighbors or accepted Nicean Christianity. Arians also continued to exist in North Africa, Spain and portions of Italy, until finally suppressed during the sixth and seventh centuries.

During the Protestant Reformation, a Polish sect known as the Polish Brethren were often referred to as Arians, due to their rejection of the Trinity.[34]

Arianism today

A modern English church called the Holy Catholic and Apostolic Church claims to follow Arian teachings, canonizing Arius on June 16, 2006.[35] However, they do not accept the Virgin Birth and bodily resurrection of Jesus Christ,[36] which places them in opposition to Arius himself, who accepted both. Furthermore, their "Arian Catholic Creed"[36] is a modern creation, not an ancient statement of faith.

Members of the congregation of Jehovah's Witnesses are sometimes referred to as "modern-day Arians", usually by their opponents. However, the Witnesses differ from Arians by saying that the Son can fully know the Father (something Arius himself denied), and by their denial of literal personality to the Holy Spirit (Arius considered the Holy Spirit to be a person or a high angel, whereas the Witnesses consider the Holy Spirit to be God's divine breath or active force). Arians generally worshipped and prayed to Jesus as God, while the Witnesses, though they do reverence Jesus as God's Son and Messiah, do not give Him the same kind of worship as they give to God the Father.

Members of The Church of Jesus Christ of Latter-day Saints (the "Mormons") are sometimes accused of being Arians by their detractors. However, the Christology of the LDS religion differs in several significant aspects from Arian theology.

Arius's doctrine

In explaining his actions against Arius, Alexander of Alexandria wrote a letter to Alexander of Constantinople and Eusebius of Nicomedia (where the emperor was then residing), detailing the errors into which he believed Arius had fallen. According to Alexander, Arius taught:

That God was not always the Father, but that there was a period when he was not the Father; that the Word of God was not from eternity, but was made out of nothing; for that the ever-existing God ('the I AM'— the eternal One) made him who did not previously exist, out of nothing; wherefore there was a time when he did not exist, inasmuch as the Son is a creature and a work. That he is neither like the Father as it regards his essence, nor is by nature either the Father's true Word, or true Wisdom, but indeed one of his works and creatures, being erroneously called Word and Wisdom, since he was himself made of God's own Word and the Wisdom which is in God, whereby God both made all things and him also. Wherefore he is as to his nature mutable and susceptible of change, as all other rational creatures are: hence the Word is alien to and other than the essence of God; and the Father is inexplicable by the Son, and invisible to him, for neither does the Word perfectly and accurately know the Father, neither can he distinctly see him. The Son knows not the nature of his own essence: for he was made on our account, in order that God might create us by him, as by an instrument; nor would he ever have existed, unless God had wished to create us.[41]

Alexander also refers to Arius's poetical *Thalia*:

God has not always been Father; there was a moment when he was alone, and was not yet Father: later he became so. The Son is not from eternity; he came from nothing.

The *Logos*

This question of the exact relationship between the Father and the Son (a part of the theological science of Christology) had been raised some fifty years before Arius, when Paul of Samosata was deposed in 269 for agreeing with those who used the word homoousios (Greek for same substance) to express the relation between the Father and the Son. This term was thought at that time to have a Sabellian tendency, though—as events showed—this was on account of its scope not having been satisfactorily defined.[43] In the discussion which followed Paul's deposition, Dionysius, the Bishop of Alexandria, used much the same language as Arius did later, and correspondence survives in which Pope Dionysius blames him for using such terminology. Dionysius responded with an explanation widely interpreted as vacillating. The Synod of Antioch, which condemned Paul of Samosata, had expressed its disapproval of the word *homoousios* in one sense, while Bishop Alexander undertook its defense in another. Although the controversy seemed to be leaning toward the opinions later championed by Arius, no firm decision had been made on the subject; in an atmosphere so intellectual as that of Alexandria, the debate seemed bound to resurface—and even intensify—at some point in the future.

Arius endorsed the following doctrines about The Son or The Word (*Logos*, referring to Jesus; see the Gospel of John 1:1):

1. that the Word (*Logos*) and the Father were not of the same essence (*ousia*);
2. that the Son was a created being (*ktisma* or *poiema*); and
3. that the worlds were created through him, so he must have existed before them and before all time.
4. However, there was a "once" [Arius did not use words meaning "time", such as *chronos* or *aion*] when He did not exist, before he was begotten of the Father.

The *Thalia*

According to Athanasius, Arius authored a poem called the *Thalia* ("abundance", "good cheer" or "banquet"): a summary of his views on the *Logos*. Part of this *Thalia* is quoted in Athanasius's *Four Discourses Against the Arians*:

"And so God Himself, as he really is, is inexpressible to all.

86

He alone has no equal, no one similar ('homoios'), and no one of the same glory.
We call Him unbegotten, in contrast to him who by nature is begotten.
We praise Him as without beginning, in contrast to him who has a beginning.
We worship Him as timeless, in contrast to him who in time has come to exist.
He who is without beginning made the Son a beginning of created things. He produced him as a son for Himself, by begetting him.
He [the Son] has none of the distinct characteristics of God's own being ('kat' hypostasis')
For he is not equal to, nor is he of the same being ('homoousios') as Him."

Also from the *Thalia*:

"At God's will the Son has the greatness and qualities that he has.
His existence from when and from whom and from then—are all from God.
He, though strong God, praises in part ('ek merous') his superior".

Thus, said Arius, God's first thought was the creation of <u>Jesus Christ</u>, therefore <u>time</u> started with the creation of the *Logos* or Word in Heaven.

In this portion of the *Thalia*, Arius endeavors to explain the ultimate incomprehensibility of the Father to the Son:

"In brief, God is inexpressible to the Son.
For He is in himself what He is, that is, indescribable,
So that the Son does not comprehend any of these things or have the understanding to explain them.
For it is impossible for him to fathom the Father, who is by Himself.

87

For the Son himself does not even know his own essence ('ousia').
For being Son, his existence is most certainly at the will of the Father.
What reasoning allows, that he who is from the Father should comprehend and know his own parent?
For clearly that which has a beginning is not able to conceive of or grasp the existence of that which has no beginning".

Here, Arius explains how the Son could still be <u>God</u>, even if he did not exist eternally:

"Understand that the Monad [eternally] was; but the Dyad was not before it came into existence.
It immediately follows that, although the Son did not exist, the Father was still God.
Hence the Son, not being [eternal] came into existence by the Father's will,
He [the Son] is the Only-begotten God, and this one is alien from [all] others."

Existing writings

Three surviving letters attributed to Arius are his letter to <u>Alexander of Alexandria</u>, his letter to <u>Eusebius of Nicomedia</u>, and his confession to Constantine. In addition, several <u>letters</u> addressed by others to Arius survive, together with brief quotations contained within the polemical works of his opponents. These quotations are often short and taken out of context, and it is difficult to tell how accurately they quote him or represent his true thinking.

Arius' *Thalia* (literally, "Festivity"), a popularized work combining prose and verse, survives in quoted fragmentary form. The two available references from this work are recorded by his opponent Athanasius: the first is a report of Arius's teaching in *Orations Against the Arians*, 1:5-6. This paraphrase has negative comments interspersed throughout, so it is difficult to consider it as being completely reliable. The second quotation is found in the document *On the Councils of*

Arminum and Seleucia, pg. 15. This passage is entirely in irregular verse, and seems to be a direct quotation or a compilation of quotations; it may have been written by someone other than Athanasius, perhaps even a person sympathetic to Arius. This second quotation does not contain several statements usually attributed to Arius by his opponents, is in metrical form, and resembles other passages that have been attributed to Arius. It also contains some positive statements about the Son. But although these quotations seem reasonably accurate, their proper context is lost, thus their place in Arius' larger system of thought is impossible to reconstruct.

Constantine I

Constantine I also supported the separation of the date of Easter from the Jewish Passover (see also Quartodecimanism), stating in his letter after the First Council of Nicaea:

"... it appeared an unworthy thing that in the celebration of this most holy feast we should follow the practice of the Jews, who have impiously defiled their hands with enormous sin, and are, therefore, deservedly afflicted with blindness of soul. ... Let us then have nothing in common with the detestable Jewish crowd; for we have received from our Saviour a different way."

Theodoret's *Ecclesiastical History* records *The Epistle of the Emperor Constantine I, concerning the matters transacted at the Council, addressed to those Bishops who were not present*:

"It was, in the first place, declared improper to follow the custom of the Jews in the celebration of this holy festival, because, their hands having been stained with crime, the minds of these wretched men are necessarily blinded. ... Let us, then, have nothing in common with the Jews, who are our adversaries. ... Let us ... studiously avoiding all contact with that evil way. ... For how can they entertain right views on any point who, after having compassed the death of the Lord, being out of their minds, are guided not by sound reason, but by an unrestrained passion, wherever their innate madness carries them. ... lest your pure minds should appear to share in the customs of a people so utterly depraved. ... Therefore, this irregularity must be corrected, in order that

89

we may no more have any thing in common with those parricides and the murderers of our Lord. ... no single point in common with the perjury of the Jews."

The First Council of Nicaea was convened by Constantine I upon the recommendations of a synod led by Hosius of Cordoba in the Eastertide of 325. This synod had been charged with investigation of the trouble brought about by the Arian controversy in the Greek-speaking east. To most bishops, the teachings of Arius were heretical and dangerous to the salvation of souls. In the summer of 325, the bishops of all provinces were summoned to Nicaea (now known as İznik, in modern-day Turkey), a place easily accessible to the majority of delegates, particularly those of Asia Minor, Syria, Palestine, Egypt, Greece, and Thrace.

This was the first general council in the history of the Church since the Apostolic Council of Jerusalem, which had established the conditions upon which Gentiles could join the Church. In the Council of Nicaea, "the Church had taken her first great step to define doctrine more precisely in response to a challenge from a heretical theology."

The long-term effects of the Council of Nicaea were significant. For the first time, representatives of many of the bishops of the Church convened to agree on a doctrinal statement. Also for the first time, the Emperor played a role, by calling together the bishops under his authority, and using the power of the state to give the Council's orders effect.

In the short-term, however, the council did not completely solve the problems it was convened to discuss and a period of conflict and upheaval continued for some time. Constantine himself was succeeded by two Arian Emperors in the Eastern Empire: his son, Constantius II and Valens. Valens could not resolve the outstanding ecclesiastical issues, and unsuccessfully confronted St. Basil over the Nicene Creed. Pagan powers within the Empire sought to maintain and at times re-establish paganism into the seat of the Emperor (see Arbogast and Julian the Apostate). Arians and Meletians soon regained nearly all of the rights they had lost, and consequently, Arianism continued to spread and to cause division in the Church during the remainder of the fourth century. Almost immediately, Eusebius of Nicomedia, an Arian bishop and cousin to Constantine I, used his influence at court to sway Constantine's favor from the orthodox Nicene bishops to the Arians. Eustathius of Antioch was deposed and exiled in 330. Athanasius, who had succeeded Alexander as Bishop of Alexandria, was deposed by the First Synod of Tyre in 335 and Marcellus of Ancyra followed him in 336. Arius himself returned to Constantinople to be readmitted into the Church, but died shortly before he could be received. Constantine died the next year, after finally receiving baptism from Arian Bishop Eusebius of Nicomedia, and "with his passing the first round in the battle after the Council of Nicaea was ended."

The Doctrine of the Trinity

The Christian doctrine of the **Trinity** teaches the unity of Father, Son, and Holy Spirit as three persons in one Godhead. The doctrine states that God is the **Triune God**, existing as three *persons*, or in the Greek *hypostases*, but one being. (Personhood in the Trinity does not match the common Western understanding of "person" as used in the English language—it does not imply an "individual, self-actualized center of free will and conscious activity." To the ancients, personhood "was in some sense individual, but always in community as well." Each *person* is understood as having the one identical essence or nature, not merely similar natures.) Since the beginning of the third century the doctrine of the Trinity has been stated as "the one God exists in three Persons and one substance, Father, Son, and Holy Spirit." *Trinitarianism*, belief in the Trinity, is a mark of Roman Catholicism, Eastern and Oriental Orthodoxy as well as of the "mainstream traditions" arising from the Protestant Reformation, such as Anglicanism, Methodism, Lutheranism and Presbyterianism. *The Oxford Dictionary of the Christian Church* describes the Trinity as "the central dogma of Christian theology"

This doctrine contrasts with Nontrinitarian positions which include Binitarianism (one deity/two persons), Unitarianism (one deity/one person), the Oneness belief held by certain Pentecostal groups. Modalism, and The Church of Jesus Christ of Latter-day Saints' view of

91

the Godhead as three separate beings who are one in purpose rather than essence.

The New Testament does not have an explicit doctrine of the Trinity. However, Southern Baptist theologian Frank Stagg emphasizes that the New Testament *does* repeatedly speak of the Father, the Son, and the Holy Spirit to "compel a trinitarian understanding of God." The doctrine developed from the biblical language used in New Testament passages such as the baptismal formula in Matthew 28:19 and took substantially its present form by the end of the 4th century as a result of controversies in which some theologians, when speaking of God, used terms such as "person", "nature", "essence", "substance", terms that had never been used by the Apostolic Fathers, in a way that the Church authorities considered to be erroneous.

Some deny that the doctrine that developed in the fourth century was based on Christian ideas, and hold instead that it was a deviation from Early Christian teaching on the nature of God or even that it was borrowed from a pre-Christian conception of a divine trinity held by Plato.

Trinitarian Etymology

The English word *Trinity* is derived from <u>Latin</u> *Trinitas*, meaning "the number three, a triad".This abstract noun is formed from the adjective *trinus* (three each, threefold, triple), as the word *unitas* is the abstract noun formed from *unus* (one).

The corresponding word in <u>Greek</u> is *Τριάς*, meaning "a set of three" or "the number three".The first recorded use of this Greek word in Christian theology (though not about the Divine Trinity) was by <u>Theophilus of Antioch</u> in about 170. He wrote: "In like manner also the three days which were before the luminaries, are <u>types</u> of the Trinity [Τριάδος], of God, and <u>His Word</u>, and <u>His wisdom</u>. And the fourth is the type of man, who needs light, that so there may be God, the Word, wisdom, man."[18]

<u>Tertullian</u>, a Latin theologian who wrote in the early third century, is credited with using the words "Trinity","person" and "substance" to explain that the Father, Son and Holy Spirit are "one in essence—not one in Person".

About a century later, in 325, the <u>First Council of Nicaea</u> established the doctrine of the Trinity as <u>orthodoxy</u> and adopted the <u>Nicene Creed</u>, which described Christ as "God of God, Light of Light, very God of very God, begotten, not made, being of one substance (*homoousios*) with the Father".

The <u>New Testament</u> does not use the word "Τριάς" (Trinity) nor explicitly teach it, but provides the material upon which the doctrine of the Trinity is based. It required reflection by the earliest Christians on the <u>earthly ministry of Jesus</u> and of what they believed to be the presence and power of God among them, which they called the Holy Spirit; and it associated the Father, Son, and Holy Spirit in such passages as the <u>Great Commission</u>: "Go therefore and make <u>disciples</u> of all nations, <u>baptizing</u> them in the name of the Father and of the Son and of the Holy Spirit"[Matt. 28:19] and <u>Paul the Apostle</u>'s blessing: "The grace of the Lord Jesus Christ and the <u>love of God</u> and the fellowship of the Holy Spirit be with you all,"[2 Cor. 13:14] while at the same time not contradicting the Jewish Shema Yisrael: "Hear, O Israel: the Lord our God, the Lord is one."[Deuteronomy 6:4][1] Apart from the passages that speak of Father Son and Holy Spirit, there are many passages that refer to God and Jesus without also referring to the Spirit.

According to Christian tradition the Trinity was introduced by the Gospels and Jesus Christ[24] "Therefore go and make disciples of all nations, baptizing them *in the name of the Father and of the Son and of the Holy Spirit,* and teaching them to obey everything I have commanded you."[Matt. 28:19-20] Jesus thus mentions the Father, the Son, and the Holy Spirit in a phrase that may suggest that there is one name that encompasses all three.

The Old Testament refers to God's word, his spirit, and Wisdom. These have been interpreted as foreshadowings of the doctrine of the Trinity, as have been also narratives such as the appearance of the three men to Abraham.[Gen. 18] Some Church Fathers believed that a knowledge of the mystery was granted to the prophets and saints of the "Old Dispensation" (in contrast to the New Covenant?), and that they identified the divine messenger of Genesis 16:7, 21:17, 31:11, Exodus 3:2 and Wisdom of the sapiential books with the Son, and "the spirit of the Lord" with the Holy Spirit. However, it is generally agreed that it would go beyond the intention and spirit of the Old Testament to correlate these notions directly with later Trinitarian doctrine. The Gospel of John opens by declaring, as usually translated: "In the beginning was the Word, and the Word was with God, *and the Word was God.* He was with God in the beginning. Through him all things were made; without him nothing was made that has been made." The rest of John 1 makes it clear that "the Word" refers to Jesus Christ. Thus John introduces a seemingly impossible contradiction, that Jesus both "was with God" and "was God" at the same time, and that was true from the beginning of creation. John also portrays Jesus Christ as the creator of the universe, such that "without him nothing was made that has been made."[John 1:3]

The Apostle John is identified as the "one whom Jesus loved" thus perhaps being the closest Apostle to Jesus. Jesus also instructed John to adopt Jesus' mother Mary as John's own in Mary's old age[Jn 19:26] such that John would have had the entire knowledge of Jesus' family when writing his Gospel. Some scholars question this, however, as the gospel of John is believed to have been written no earlier than the last decade of the first century (ca. 96 CE, according to Catholic tradition).

Jesus frequently referred to the "Father" as God as distinct from himself, but also discussed "The Holy Spirit" as a being distinct from either God the Father or Jesus himself.

These things I have spoken to you while abiding with you. But the Helper, the Holy Spirit, whom the Father will send in My name, he will teach you all things, and bring to your remembrance all that I said to you.

– John 14:25-26

In this passage, Jesus portrays the Father sending the Holy Spirit—that is the Father and the Holy Spirit are two distinctly different persons, and portrays both the Father and the Holy Spirit as distinct from Jesus himself. Thus even apart from whether Jesus was God, Jesus declares that the Father and the Holy Spirit are two different persons, both of them divine. In the same way, the Old Testament frequently refers to "the Spirit of God" as something slightly different from God himself.

The fourth Gospel also elaborates on the role of Holy Spirit, sent as an advocate for believers. The immediate context of these verses was providing "assurance of the presence and power of God both in the ministry of Jesus and the ongoing life of the community"; but, beyond this immediate context, these verses raised questions of relationship between Father, Son and the Holy Spirit, especially as concerns their distinction and their unity. These questions were hotly debated over the ensuing centuries, and mainstream Christianity resolved the issues by drawing up creeds.

However, some scholars dispute the authenticity of the Trinity and argue that the doctrine is the result of "later theological interpretations of Christ's nature and function." The concept was expressed in early writings from the beginning of the second century forward. Some believe the concept was introduced in the Old Testament book of Isaiah written around 700 years before Jesus, copies of which were preserved from 300 years before Jesus in the Dead Sea Scrolls. Isaiah 9:6

prophesies "For unto us a Child is born, Unto us a Son is given; And the government will be upon his shoulder. And his name will be called Wonderful Counselor, Mighty God, Everlasting Father, Prince of Peace." Thus a son who will be born at a particular point in history (to a virgin or young woman[Isa. 7:14] is also "Mighty God, Everlasting Father". This is the Christian teaching that God exists simultaneously as the Eternal God and also as a Son (Jesus) born to a virgin. Isaiah refers to the Son as "Mighty God, Everlasting Father".

Various passages from the Christian and Hebrew scriptures have been cited as supporting this doctrine, while other passages are cited as opposing it.

Scriptural texts cited as implying support

The diverse references to God, Jesus, and the Spirit found in the New Testament were later systematized into a Trinity—one God subsisting in three persons and one substance—to combat heretical tendencies of how the three are related and to defend the church against charges of worshiping two or three gods. The doctrine was not explicitly stated in the New Testament and no New Testament writer expounds on the relationship among the three in the detail that later writers do. Thus, while Matthew records a special connection between God the Father and Jesus the Son,[Matt. 11:27] he falls short of claiming that Jesus is equal with God[Matt. 24:36][32] although John is more explicit and writes that Jesus Christ told the Jews: "I and the Father are one".[John 10:30]

The most influential New Testament text was the reference to the three Persons in the baptismal formula in Matthew 28:19. Other passages also were seen as having Trinitarian overtones, such as the Pauline benediction of 2 Cor. 13:14. The Gospel of John starts, as generally understood and translated, with the affirmation that in the beginning Jesus as Word "was with God and ...was God",[John 1:1] and ends with Thomas's confession of faith to Jesus, "My Lord and my God!"[John 20:28][32] There is no significant tendency among modern scholars to deny that these two verses identify Jesus with God. The same Gospel also suggests that Jesus' use of the term "Son of God" inferred essential equality and unity of Father and Son—"...making himself equal to the Father"[John 5:18] [19:7] and saying "I and the Father arc one."[10:30] John also suggests a hierarchy when Jesus is quoted as saying, "The Father is greater than I,"[14:28] a statement appealed to by Marcionism, Valentinianism, Arianism who held non-trinitarian views. Summarizing the role of scripture in the formation of Trinitarian belief, Gregory Nazianzen argues in his *Orations* that the revelation was intentionally gradual:

> "The Old Testament proclaimed the Father openly, and the Son more obscurely. The New manifested the Son, and suggested the deity of the Spirit. Now the Spirit himself dwells among us, and supplies us with a clearer demonstration of himself. For it was not safe, when the Godhead of the Father was not yet acknowledged, plainly to proclaim the Son; nor when that of the Son was not yet received to burden us further."

References to Father, Son, and Holy Spirit

A few verses directly reference the Father, Son, and Holy Spirit at the same time:

- "As soon as Jesus Christ was baptized, he went up out of the water. At that moment heaven was opened, and he saw the Spirit of God descending like a dove and landing on him. And a voice from heaven said, 'This is my Son, whom I love; with him I am well pleased.'"[Matt. 3:16–17] [Mark 1:10–11] [Luke 3:22] [John 1:32]
- "The angel answered and said to her, 'The Holy Spirit will come upon you, and the power of the Most High will overshadow you; and for that reason the holy Child shall be called the Son of God.'"[Luke 1:35]
- "How much more, then, will the blood of Christ, who through the eternal Spirit offered himself unblemished to God, cleanse our consciences from acts that lead to death, so that we may serve the living God!"[Heb. 9:14]

- "But Stephen, full of the Holy Spirit, looked up to heaven and saw the glory of God, and Jesus standing at the right hand of God." [Acts 7:55]
- This passage contains many complex formulations of the relationship between God, Christ, and Spirit, including "the Spirit of him who raised Jesus from the dead,"[Rom. 8:11] "all who are led by the Spirit of God are sons of God,"[8:14-17] and "the Spirit intercedes for the saints according to the will of God."[8:26-27]

Some even reference these as part of a single formula:

- "Therefore go and make disciples of all nations, baptizing them in the name of the Father and of the Son and of the Holy Spirit"[Matt. 28:19] (see Trinitarian formula). It has been claimed that writings of Eusebius show the mention of Father, Son, and Holy Spirit to have displaced a request by Jesus that his disciples baptize people in his name but all manuscripts of the Gospel of Matthew contain, without any variation, the mention of the Trinity.
- "The grace of the Lord Jesus Christ and the love of God and the fellowship of the Holy Spirit be with all of you." [2 Cor. 13:14]

Comma Johanneum

In addition to these, 1 John 5:7, which is found in the King James Version but not in modern English translations nor in the official Latin text (a revision of the Vulgate) of the Roman Catholic Church, states: "For there are three that bear record in heaven, the Father, the Word, and the Holy Ghost: and these three are one." However, this Comma Johanneum is not considered to be part of the genuine text. It is commonly found in Latin manuscripts, but is absent from the Greek manuscripts, except for a few late examples, where the passage appears to have been back-translated from the Latin. Erasmus, the compiler of the *Textus Receptus*, on which the King James Version was based, noticed that the passage was not found in any of the Greek manuscripts at his disposal and refused to include it until presented with a manuscript containing it, while still suspecting, as is now agreed, that the phrase was a gloss. Although the Latin Church Father, Saint Cyprian, alone among early writers, is thought to have referred to the passage, it is now considered not to be part of the original text.

Jesus as God

In the New Testament, the Gospel of John has been seen as aimed at emphasizing Jesus' divinity, presenting Jesus as the Logos, pre-existent and divine, from its first words, "In the beginning was the Word, and the Word was with God, and the Word was God";[John 1:1] and "The Word became flesh and made his dwelling among us. We have seen his glory, the glory of the One and Only, who came from the Father, full of grace and truth."[1:14][45] Other passages of John's Gospel interpreted in this sense include "before Abraham was born, I am!",[8:58] "I and the Father are one",[10:30] "The Father is in me, and I in the Father",[10:38] and "Thomas said to him, 'My Lord and my God!'"[20:28] [46] John is also seen to identify Jesus as the Lord whom Isaiah saw,[Jn. 12:34-45] [Isa. 6:1-10] while other texts[Heb. 1:1-12] are also understood as referring to Jesus as God.

Expressions also in the Pauline epistles have been interpreted as attributing divinity to Jesus. They include Colossians 1:16 ("For by him all things were created: things in heaven and on earth, visible and invisible, whether thrones or powers or rulers or authorities; all things were created by him and for him") and 2:9 ("For in Christ all the fullness of the Deity lives in bodily form"), and in Paul the Apostle's claim in Galatians 1:1 to have been "sent not from men nor by man, but by Jesus Christ and God the Father".Another biblical demonstration of Jesus as God comes from English abolitionist and philanthropist Granville Sharp who noticed the following Greek idiom, which is now called Granville Sharp's rule: when two nouns that are personal, singular, and not proper names are connected in a TSKS pattern (The—Substantive—Kai—Substantive, where 'kai' is Greek for 'and') then the two nouns refer to the same person. Obviously this idiom does not apply to proper names—the phrase "The Pope and Mr. Gorbachev" refers to two separate people. Passages like Titus 2:13 and 2 Peter 1:1 fit this pattern. Therefore, when Paul says:[Titus 2:13] "The great God and savior, Jesus Christ" he is grammatically identifying Jesus Christ as the great God. Proper nouns are not used in this phrase. Capitalized in

English, the word God in Greek grammar is not a proper noun. While 'Jesus Christ' here is a proper noun it is the word 'savior' that is in the TSKS construction. In his review of over 1,000 years of Greek literature, Christopher Wordsworth confirmed that early church Fathers had this same understanding of the text. He writes, "I have observed...some hundreds of instances of the 'The great God and savior';[Titus 2:13] and no fewer than several thousand of the form 'The God and savior'"[2 Pet. 1:1] and in every case (when it could be determined) they spoke "only of one person." This Greek idiom shows that both the New Testament authors and the early church Fathers considered Jesus to be God.

It is agreed that the Bible also refers to Jesus as a man, which is in line with the Trinitarian theological concept of kenosis.

Claims of Old Testament precedents to Trinitarian doctrine

Genesis 18–19 have been interpreted by Christians as a Trinitarian text. The narrative has the Lord appearing to Abraham, who was visited by three men.[Gen. 18:1-2] Then in Genesis 19, "the two angels" visited Lot at Sodom. The interplay between Abraham on the one hand, and the Lord/three men/the two angels on the other was an intriguing text for those who believed in a single God in three persons. Justin Martyr, and John Calvin similarly, interpreted it such that Abraham was visited by God, who was accompanied by two angels. Justin supposed that the god who visited Abraham was distinguishable from the god who remains in the heavens, but was nevertheless identified as the (monotheistic) god. Justin appropriated the god who visited Abraham to Jesus, the second person of the Trinity.

Augustine, in contrast, held that the three visitors to Abraham were the three persons of the Trinity. He saw no indication that the visitors were unequal, as would be the case in Justin's reading. Then in Genesis 19, two of the visitors were addressed by Lot in the singular: "Lot said to them, 'Not so, my lord.'" Augustine saw that Lot could address them as one because they had a single substance, despite the plurality of persons.Some Christians see indications in the Old Testament of a plurality and unity in God, an idea that is rejected by Judaism, which

100

interprets the New Testament also as not including the doctrine. Some Christians interpret the theophanies or appearances of the Angel of the Lord as revelations of a person distinct from God, who is nonetheless called God. This interpretation is found in Christianity as early as Justin Martyr and Melito of Sardis, and reflects ideas that were already present in Philo. The Old Testament theophanies were thus seen as Christophanies, each a "preincarnate appearance of the Messiah".God is not directly identified as "the Son" in the Old Testament. Israel (and, poetically Ephraim) are called God's first born son, representing an aspect of the Jewish nation's relationship with God. There are, however, what many Christians believe are foreshadowings of Jesus as God the Son.

Psalm 2 is widely considered a Messianic psalm prophetically describing the Lord's "Anointed One" (verse 2). It contains in verse 7 the divine decree: "You are my son, today I have become your Father." Verse 12 contains the words "Kiss the son". While in verse 7 the Hebrew word for son is used, in verse 12 a Chaldean word is used. Support for the translation of the Chaldean word as "son" is found in its other appearances.[cf.[Ezra 5:2]] This psalm denotes a Father—Son relationship between God and "the Anointed One", one who would receive the nations as his heritage (verse 8). Isaiah 9, also considered a Messianic prophecy, describes the coming Messiah as "Mighty God" (verse 6). Psalm 110 describes the LORD (understood as God the Father) sharing his eternal glory with the psalmist's Lord (understood to be the Son, the Messiah).

In Daniel 7 the prophet records his vision of "one like a son of man, coming with the clouds of heaven", who "was given authority, glory and sovereign power; all peoples, nations and men of every language worshiped him" (v. 14). Christians believe that worship is only properly given to God, and that considering other Bible passages this "son of man" can be identified as the second person of the Trinity. Parallels may be drawn between Daniel's vision and Jesus' words to the Jewish high priest that in the future those assembled would see "the son of Man sitting at the right hand of the Mighty One and coming on the clouds of heaven."[Matt. 26:64-65] Jesus was immediately accused of blasphemy, as at other times when he had identified his oneness with God.[John 10:33] Christians also believe that John saw the resurrected, gloried Jesus and described him as "One like the Son of Man."[Rev. 1:13]

101

History of the doctrines of the Trinity

Origin of the formula

The basis for the doctrine of the Trinity is found in New Testament passages that associate the Father, Son, and Holy Spirit. Two such passages are Matthew's Great Commission: "Go therefore and make disciples of all nations, baptizing them in the name of the Father and of the Son and of the Holy Spirit"[Matt 28:19] and St Paul's: "The grace of the Lord Jesus Christ and the love of God and the fellowship of the Holy Spirit be with you all."[2 Cor. 13:14]

In 325, the Council of Nicaea adopted a term for the relationship between the Son and the Father that from then on was seen as the hallmark of orthodoxy; it declared that the Son is "of the same substance" (ὁμοούσιος) as the Father. This was further developed into the formula "three persons, one substance". The answer to the question "*What* is God?" indicates the one-ness of the divine nature, while the answer to the question "*Who* is God?" indicates the three-ness of "Father, Son and Holy Spirit". Saint Athanasius, who was a participant in the Council, stated that the bishops were forced to use this terminology, which is not found in Scripture, because the Biblical phrases that they would have preferred to use were claimed by the Arians to be capable of being interpreted in what the bishops considered to be a heretical sense. They therefore "commandeered the non-scriptural term *homoousios* ('of one substance') to safeguard the essential relation of the Son to the Father that had been denied by Arius."

The Confession of the Council of Nicaea said little about the Holy Spirit. The doctrine of the divinity and personality of the Holy Spirit was developed by Athanasius (*c* 293–373) in the last decades of his life. He defended and refined the Nicene formula. By the end of the 4th century, under the leadership of Basil of Caesarea, Gregory of Nyssa, and Gregory of Nazianzus (the Cappadocian Fathers), the doctrine had reached substantially its current form.

Formulation of the doctrine

The most significant developments were articulated in the 4th century by the Church Fathers. Although the earliest Church Fathers had affirmed the teachings of the Apostles, their focus was on their pastoral duties to the Church under the persecution of the Roman Empire. Thus the early Fathers were largely unable to compose doctrinal treatises and theological expositions. With the relaxing of the persecution of the church during the rise of Constantine, the stage was set for ecumenical dialogue.

Trinitarians believe that the resultant councils and creeds did not discover or create doctrine, but rather, responding to serious heresies such as Arianism, articulated in the creeds the truths that the orthodox church had believed since the time of the apostles.

The Ante-Nicene Fathers, although likely foreign to the specifics of Trinitarian theology because they were not defined until the 4th century, nevertheless affirmed Christ's deity and referenced "Father, Son and Holy Spirit". Trinitarians view these as elements of the codified doctrine.

The Trinitarian view has been affirmed as an article of faith by the Nicene (325/381) and Athanasian creeds (circa 500), which attempted to standardize belief in the face of disagreements on the subject. These creeds were formulated and ratified by the Church of the third and fourth centuries in reaction to heterodox theologies concerning the Trinity and/or Christ. The Nicene-Constantinopolitan Creed, revised in 381 by the second of these councils, is professed by the Eastern Orthodox Church and, with one addition (Filioque clause), the Roman Catholic Church, and has been retained in some form in the Anglican Communion and most Protestant denominations.

The Nicene Creed, which is a classic formulation of the doctrine of the Trinity, uses "homoousios" (Greek for "of *the same* essence") of the relation of the Son's relationship with the Father. This word differs from that used by non-Trinitarians of the time, "homoiousios" (Greek for "of *similar* essence"), by a single Greek letter, "one iota", a fact proverbially used to speak of deep divisions, especially in theology, expressed by seemingly small verbal differences.

One of the (probably three) Church councils that in 264–266 condemned Paul of Samosata for his Adoptionist theology also condemned the term "homoousios" in the sense he used it. Fourth-century Christians who objected to the Nicene trinity made copious use of this condemnation by a reputable council. Moreover, the meanings of "ousia" and "hypostasis" overlapped then, so that the latter term for some meant *essence* and for others *person*. Athanasius of Alexandria (293–373) helped to clarify the terms.

Because Christianity converts cultures from within, the doctrinal formulas as they have developed bear the marks of the ages through which the church has passed. The rhetorical tools of Greek philosophy, especially of Neoplatonism, are evident in the language adopted to explain the church's rejection of Arianism and Adoptionism on one hand (teaching that Christ is inferior to the Father, or even that he was merely human), and Docetism and Sabellianism on the other hand (teaching that Christ was an illusion, or that he was identical to God the Father). Augustine of Hippo has been noted at the forefront of these formulations; and he contributed much to the speculative development of the doctrine of the Trinity as it is known today, in the West; the Cappadocian Fathers (Basil the Great, Gregory of Nyssa, and Gregory Nazianzus) are more prominent in the East. The imprint of Augustinianism is found, for example, in the western Athanasian Creed, which, although it bears the name and reproduces the views of the fourth century opponent of Arianism, was probably written much later.

These controversies were for most purposes settled at the Ecumenical councils, whose creeds affirm the doctrine of the Trinity.

Modalists attempted to resolve the mystery of the Trinity by holding that the Father, the Son and the Holy Ghost are modes, aspects or roles, of God. This anti-Trinitarian view contends that the three "persons" are not distinct persons, but titles which describe how humanity has interacted with or experienced God. In the role of the Father, God is the provider and creator of all. In the mode of the Son, man experiences God in the flesh, as a human, fully man and fully God. God manifests as the Holy Spirit by his actions on Earth and within the lives of Christians. This view is known as Sabellianism, and was rejected as heresy by the Ecumenical Councils although it is still prevalent today among those denominations known as "Oneness" and "Apostolic" Pentecostal Christians, the largest of which is the United Pentecostal Church International (see below, under "Nontrinitarianism"). Trinitarianism, on the other hand, insists that the Father, Son and Spirit simultaneously exist as three persons in one essence, each fully the same God.

The doctrine developed into its present form precisely through this confrontation with alternatives; and refinement continues in the same way. Even now, ecumenical dialogue between Eastern Orthodox, Oriental Orthodox, Roman Catholic, the Assyrian Church of the East, Anglican and Trinitarian Protestants, seeks an expression of Trinitarian and Christological doctrine which will overcome the extremely subtle differences that have largely contributed to dividing them into separate communities. The doctrine of the Trinity is therefore symbolic, paradoxically, of division and unity.

Trinitarian theology

Baptism as the beginning lesson

Baptism is generally conferred with the Trinitarian formula, "in the name of the Father, and of the Son, and of the Holy Spirit."[Matt. 28:19] Trinitarians identify this name with the Christian faith into which baptism is an initiation, as seen for example in the statement of Basil the Great (330–379): "We are bound to be baptized in the terms we have received, and to profess faith in the terms in which we have been baptized." "This is the Faith of our baptism", the First Council of Constantinople also says (382), "that teaches us to believe in the Name of the Father, of the Son and of the Holy Spirit. According to this Faith there is one Godhead, Power, and Being of the Father, of the Son, and of the Holy Spirit."

Matthew 28:19 may be taken to indicate that baptism was associated with this Trinitarian formula from the earliest decades of the Church's existence.

Some groups, such as Oneness Pentecostals, demur from the Trinitarian view on baptism. For them, the omission of the formula in Acts outweighs all other considerations, and is a liturgical guide for their own practice. For this reason, they often focus on the baptisms in Acts, citing many authoritative theological works. For example, Kittel is cited where he is speaking of the phrase "in the name" (Greek: εἰς τὸ ὄνομα) as used in the baptisms recorded in Acts:

> "The distinctive feature of Christian baptism is that it is administered in Christ (εἰς Χριστόν), or in the name of Christ (εἰς τὸ ὄνομα Χριστοῦ). (Gerhard Kittel, *Theological Dictionary of the New Testament* (Grand Rapids: Eerdmans, 1977), 1:539.)
>
> The formula (εἰς τὸ ὄνομα) seems to have been a tech. term in Hellenistic commerce ("to the account"). In both cases the use of the phrase is understandable, since the account bears the name of the one who owns it, and in baptism the name of Christ is pronounced, invoked and confessed by the one who baptises or the one baptised[Acts 22:16] or both." (Kittel, 1:540.)

"Those who place great emphasis on the baptisms in Acts often likewise question the authenticity of Matthew 28:19 in its present form. A. Ploughman, apparently following F. C. Conybeare, has questioned the authenticity of Matthew 28:19, but most scholars of New Testament textual criticism accept the authenticity of the passage, since there are no variant manuscripts regarding the formula, and the extant form of the passage is attested in the Didache and other patristic works of the first and second centuries: Ignatius,[73] Tertullian, Hippolytus, Cyprian, and Gregory Thaumaturgus. The Acts of the Apostles only mentions believers being baptized "in the name of Jesus Christ"[Acts 2:38] [10:48] and "in the name of the Lord Jesus."[8:16] [19:5] There are no biblical references to baptism in the name of the Father and of the Son and of

106

the Holy Spirit outside of Matthew 28:19, nor references, biblical or patristic, to baptism in the name of (the Lord) Jesus (Christ) outside the Acts of the Apostles. Commenting on Matthew 28:19, Gerhard Kittel states:

> "This threefold relation [of Father, Son and Spirit] soon found fixed expression in the triadic formulae in 2 Cor. 13:14 and in 1 Cor. 12:4-6. The form is first found in the baptismal formula in Matthew 28:19; Did., 7. 1 and 3....[I]t is self-evident that Father, Son and Spirit are here linked in an indissoluble threefold relationship."

In the synoptic Gospels the baptism of Jesus is often interpreted as a manifestation of all three persons of the Trinity: "And when Jesus was baptized, he went up immediately from the water, and behold, the heavens were opened and he saw the spirit of God descending like a dove, and alighting on him; and lo, a voice from heaven, saying, 'This is my beloved Son, with whom I am well pleased.'"[Matt. 3:16–17]

One God (Monotheism)

Christianity is a monotheistic religion. Never in the New Testament does the trinitarian concept become a "tritheism" (three Gods) nor even two. God is one, and that the Godhead is a single being is strongly declared in the Bible:

- The *Shema* of the Hebrew Scriptures: "Hear, O Israel: the LORD our God, the LORD is one."[Deut. 6:4]
- The first of the Ten Commandments—"Thou shalt have no other gods before me"[5:7]. (A statement of Monolatrism, it is frequently cited as if it promotes Monotheism)
- and "Thus saith the LORD the King of Israel and his redeemer the LORD of hosts: I am the first and I am the last; and beside me there is no God."[Isa. 44:6]
- In the New Testament: "The Lord our God is one."[Mk. 12:29]

In the Trinitarian view, the Father and the Son and the Holy Ghost share the one essence, substance or being. The central and crucial affirmation of Christian faith is that there is one savior, God, and one salvation, manifest in Jesus Christ, to which there is access only because of the Holy Spirit. The God of the Old Testament is still the same as the God of the New. In Christianity, statements about a solitary God are intended to distinguish the Hebraic understanding from the polytheistic view, which see divine power as shared by several beings, beings which can and do disagree and have conflicts with each other.

God in three persons

According to the Trinity doctrine, God exists as three *persons*, or *hypostases*, but is one being, that is, has but a single divine nature. Chalcedonians—Roman Catholics, Orthodox Christians, Anglicans and Protestants—hold that, in addition, the second person of the Trinity— God the Son, Jesus—assumed human nature, so that he has two natures (and hence two wills), and is really and fully both true God and true human. In the Oriental Orthodox theology, the Chalcedonian formulation is rejected in favor of the position that the union of the two natures, though unconfused, births a third nature: redeemed humanity, the new creation.

The members of the Trinity are said to be co-equal and co-eternal, one in essence, nature, power, action, and will. As stated in the Athanasian Creed, the Father is uncreated, the Son is uncreated, and the Holy Spirit is uncreated, and all three are eternal with no beginning.[81] The Roman Catholic Church teaches that, in the sense of the Latin verb *procedere* (which does not have to indicate ultimate origin and is therefore compatible with proceeding *through*), but not in that of the Greek verb ἐκπορεύεσθαι (which implies ultimate origin), the Spirit "proceeds" from the Father and the Son (see Filioque), and the Eastern Orthodox Church, which teaches that the Spirit "proceeds" from the Father alone, has made no statement on the claim of a difference in meaning between the two words, one Greek and one Latin, both of which are translated as "proceeds". There is no dispute on the statement in the Nicene Creed that the Holy Spirit is worshipped together with the Father and the Son.

It has been stated that because three persons exist in God as one unity, "The Father and the Son and the Holy Spirit" are not three different names for different parts of God but one name for God, because the Father can not be divided from the Son or the Holy Spirit from the Son. God has always loved, and there has always existed perfectly harmonious communion between the three persons of the Trinity. One consequence of this teaching is that God could not have created man to have *someone to talk to* or *to love*: God "already" enjoyed personal communion; being perfect, he did not create man because of a lack or inadequacy he had. Another consequence, according to Rev. Fr. Thomas Hopko, an Eastern Orthodox theologian, is that if God were not a Trinity, he could not have loved prior to creating other beings on whom to bestow his love. Thus God says, "Let *us* make man in *our* image, in our likeness, and let them rule over the fish of the sea and the birds of the air, over the livestock, over all the earth, and over all the creatures that move along the ground. So God created man in his own image, in the image of God he created him; male and female he created them."[Gen. 1:26-27] For Trinitarians, emphasis in Genesis 1:26 is on the plurality in the Deity, and in 1:27 on the unity of the divine Essence. A possible interpretation of Genesis 1:26 is that God's relationships in the Trinity are mirrored in man by the ideal relationship between husband and wife, two persons becoming one flesh, as described in Eve's creation later in the next chapter.[2:22]

Mutually indwelling

A useful explanation of the relationship of the distinct divine persons is called "perichoresis", from Greek *going around, envelopment* (written with a long O, omega—some mistakenly associate it with the Greek word for dance, which however is spelled with a short O, omicron). This concept refers for its basis to John 14–17, where Jesus is instructing the disciples concerning the meaning of his departure. His going to the Father, he says, is for their sake; so that he might come to them when the "other comforter" is given to them. Then, he says, his disciples will dwell in him, as he dwells in the Father, and the Father dwells in him, and the Father will dwell in them. This is so, according to the theory of perichoresis, because the persons of the Trinity "reciprocally contain one another, so that one permanently envelopes and is permanently enveloped by, the other whom he yet envelopes". (Hilary of Poitiers, *Concerning the Trinity* 3:1). [1]

This co-indwelling may also be helpful in illustrating the Trinitarian conception of salvation. The first doctrinal benefit is that it effectively excludes the idea that God has parts. Trinitarians affirm that God is a simple, not an aggregate, being. The second doctrinal benefit is that it harmonizes well with the doctrine that the Christian's union with the Son in his humanity brings him into union with one who contains in himself, in St. Paul's words, "all the fullness of deity" and not a part. (*See also: Theosis*). Perichoresis provides an intuitive figure of what this might mean. The Son, the eternal Word, is from all eternity the dwelling place of God; he is the "Father's house", just as the Son dwells in the Father and the Spirit; so that, when the Spirit is "given", then it happens as Jesus said, "I will not leave you as orphans; for I will come to you."[John 14:18]

Some forms of human union are considered to be not identical but analogous to the Trinitarian concept, as found for example in Jesus' words about marriage: "For this cause shall a man leave his father and mother, and cleave to his wife; And they twain shall be one flesh: so then they are no more twain, but one flesh."[Mark 10:7–8] According to the words of Jesus, married persons are in some sense no longer two, but joined into one. Therefore, Orthodox theologians also see the marriage relationship as an image, or "icon" of the Trinity, relationships of communion in which, in the words of St. Paul, participants are "members one of another". As with marriage, the unity of the church with Christ is similarly considered in some sense analogous to the unity of the Trinity, following the prayer of Jesus to the Father, for the church, that "they may be one, even as we are one".[John 17:22]

Eternal generation and procession

Trinitarianism affirms that the Son is "begotten" (or "generated") of the Father and that the Spirit "proceeds" from the Father, but the Father is "neither begotten nor proceeds". The argument over whether the Spirit proceeds from the Father alone, or from the Father and the Son, was one of the catalysts of the Great Schism, in this case concerning the Western addition of the Filioque clause to the Nicene Creed.

This language is often considered difficult because, if used regarding humans or other created things, it would imply time and change; when used here, no beginning, change in being, or process within time is intended and is excluded. The Son is generated ("born" or "begotten"), and the Spirit proceeds, eternally. Augustine of Hippo explains, "Thy years are one day, and Thy day is not daily, but today; because Thy today yields not to tomorrow, for neither does it follow yesterday. Thy today is eternity; therefore Thou begat the Co-eternal, to whom Thou saidst, 'This day have I begotten Thee.'"[Ps. 2:7]

Son begotten, not created

Because the Son is begotten, not made, the substance of his person is that of the deity. The creation is brought into being through the Son, but the Son himself is not part of it except through his incarnation.

The church fathers used several analogies to express this thought. St. Irenaeus of Lyons was the final major theologian of the second century. He writes "the Father is God, and the Son is God, for whatever is begotten of God is God." (Compare Spinoza's philosophy of God)

Extending the analogy, it might be said, similarly, that whatever is generated (procreated) of humans is human. Thus, given that humanity is, in the words of the Bible, "created in the image and likeness of God", an analogy can be drawn between the Divine Essence and human nature, between the Divine Persons and human persons. However, given the fall, this analogy is far from perfect, even though, like the Divine Persons, human persons are characterized by being "loci of relationship". For Trinitarian Christians, this analogy is important with regard to the Church, which St. Paul calls "the body of Christ" and whose members are, because they are "members of Christ", also "members one of another".

However, an attempt to explain the mystery to some extent must break down, and has limited usefulness, being designed, not so much to fully explain the Trinity, but to point to the experience of communion with the Triune God within the Church as the Body of Christ. The difference between those who believe in the Trinity and those who do not, is not an issue of understanding the mystery. The difference is primarily one of belief concerning the personal identity of Christ. It is a difference in conception of the salvation connected with Christ that drives all reactions, either favorable or unfavorable, to the doctrine of the Holy Trinity. As it is, the doctrine of the Trinity is directly tied up with Christology.

Economic and ontological Trinity

- Economic Trinity: This refers to the acts of the triune God with respect to the creation, history, salvation, the formation of the Church, the daily lives of believers, etc. and describes how the Trinity operates within history in terms of the roles or functions performed by each Person of the Trinity—God's relationship with creation.
- Ontological (or essential or immanent) Trinity: This speaks of the interior life of the Trinity[John 1:1–2]—the reciprocal relationships of Father, Son and Spirit to each other without reference to God's relationship with creation.

Or more simply—the ontological Trinity (who God is) and the economic Trinity (what God does). Most Christians believe the economic reflects and reveals the ontological. Catholic theologian Karl Rahner went so far as to say "The 'economic' Trinity is the 'immanent' Trinity, and vice versa."

The ancient Nicene theologians argued that everything the Trinity does is done by Father, Son, and Spirit working together with one will. The three persons of the Trinity always work inseparably, for their work is always the work of the one God. Because of this unity of will, the Trinity cannot involve the eternal subordination of the Son to the Father. Eternal subordination can only exist if the Son's will is at least conceivably different from the Father's. But Nicene orthodoxy says it is not. The Son's will cannot be different from the Father's because it is the Father's. They have but one will as they have but one being.

Otherwise they would not be one God. If there were relations of command and obedience between the Father and the Son, there would be no Trinity at all but rather three gods. On this point St. Basil observes "When then He says, 'I have not spoken of myself,' and again, 'As the Father said unto me, so I speak,' and 'The word which ye hear is not mine, but [the Father's] which sent me,' and in another place, 'As the Father gave me commandment, even so I do,' it is not because He lacks deliberate purpose or power of initiation, nor yet because He has to wait for the preconcerted key-note, that he employs language of this kind. His object is to make it plain that His own will is connected in indissoluble union with the Father. Do not then let us understand by what is called a 'commandment' a peremptory mandate delivered by organs of speech, and giving orders to the Son, as to a subordinate, concerning what He ought to do. Let us rather, in a sense befitting the Godhead, perceive a transmission of will, like the reflexion of an object in a mirror, passing without note of time from Father to Son.." In explaining why the Bible speaks of the Son as being subordinate to the Father, the great theologian Athanasius argued that scripture gives a "double account" of the son of God—one of his temporal and voluntary subordination in the incarnation, and the other of his eternal divine status. For Athanasius, the Son is eternally one in being with the Father, temporally and voluntarily subordinate in his incarnate ministry. Such human traits, he argued, were not to be read back into the eternal Trinity.

Like Athanasius, the Cappadocian Fathers also insisted there was no economic inequality present within the Trinity. As Basil wrote: "We perceive the operation of the Father, Son, and Holy Spirit to be one and the same, in no respect showing differences or variation; from this identity of operation we necessarily infer the unity of nature."

Augustine also rejected an economic hierarchy within the Trinity. He claimed that the three persons of the Trinity "share the inseparable equality one substance present in divine unity".[90] Because the three persons are one in their inner life, this means that for Augustine their works in the world are one. For this reason, it is an impossibility for Augustine to speak of the Father commanding and the Son obeying as if there could be a conflict of wills within the eternal Trinity.

John Calvin also spoke at length about the doctrine of the Trinity. Like Athanasius and Augustine before him, he concluded that Philippians 2:4-11 prescribed how scripture was to be read correctly. For him the Son's obedience is limited to the incarnation and is indicative of his true humanity assumed for human salvation. Much of this work is summed up in the Athanasian Creed. This creed stresses the unity of the Trinity and the equality of the persons. It ascribes equal divinity, majesty, and authority to all three persons. All three are said to be "almighty" and "Lord" (no subordination in authority; "none is before or after another" (no hierarchical ordering); and "none is greater, or less than another" (no subordination in being or nature). Thus, since the divine persons of the Trinity act with one will, there is no possibility of hierarchy-inequality in the Trinity.

Since the 1980s, some evangelical theologians have come to the conclusion that the members of the Trinity may be economically unequal while remaining ontologically equal. This theory was put forward by George W. Knight III in his 1977 book The New Testament Teaching on the Role Relationship of Men and Women, states that the Son of God is eternally subordinated in authority to God the Father. This conclusion was used to support the main thesis of his book: that women are permanently subordinated in authority to their husbands in the home and to male leaders in the church, despite being ontologically equal. Subscribers to this theory insist that the Father has the role of giving commands and the Son has the role of obeying them.

Orthodox, Roman Catholic, Anglican, and Protestant distinctions

The Western (Roman Catholic) tradition is more prone to make positive statements concerning the relationship of persons in the Trinity. Explanations of the Trinity are not the same thing as the doctrine; nevertheless, the Augustinian West is inclined to think in philosophical terms concerning the rationality of God's being, and is prone on this basis to be more open than the East to seek philosophical formulations which make the doctrine more intelligible, while recognizing that these formulations are only analogies.

Eastern Christianity, for its part, correlates ecclesiology and Trinitarian doctrine, and seeks to understand the doctrine of the Trinity via the experience of the Church, which it understands to be "an icon of the Trinity". Therefore, when St. Paul writes concerning Christians that all are "members one of another", Eastern Christians in turn understand this as also applying to the Divine Persons.

The principal disagreement between Western and Eastern Christianity on the Trinity has been the relationship of the Holy Spirit with the other two hypostases. The original credal formulation of the Council of Constantinople was that the Holy Spirit proceeds "from the Father". While this phrase is still used unaltered both in the Eastern Churches, including the Eastern Catholic Churches, and, when the Nicene Creed is recited in Greek, in the Latin Church, it became customary in the Latin-speaking Church, beginning with the provincial Third Council of Toledo in 589, to add "and the Son" (Latin *Filioque*). Although this insertion into the Creed was explicitly rejected by Pope Leo III (who no less explicitly approved the doctrine it expressed) it was finally used in a Papal Mass by Pope Benedict VIII in 1014, thus completing its spread throughout Western Christianity. The Eastern Orthodox Churches object to it on ecclesiological and theological grounds.

The 1978 Anglican Lambeth Conference requested:

that all member Churches of the Anglican Communion should consider omitting the Filioque from the Nicene Creed, and that the Anglican-Orthodox Joint Doctrinal Commission through the Anglican Consultative Council should assist them in presenting the theological issues to their appropriate synodical bodies and should be responsible for any necessary consultation with other Churches of the Western tradition. None of the member Churches has implemented this request; but the Church of England, while keeping the phrase in the Creed recited in its own services, presents in its Common Worship series of service books a text of the creed without it for use "on suitable ecumenical occasions".

Most Protestant groups that use the creed also include the Filioque clause. However, the issue is usually not controversial among them because their conception is often less exact than is discussed above (exceptions being the Presbyterian <u>Westminster Confession</u> 2:3, the <u>London Baptist Confession</u> 2:3, and the Lutheran <u>Augsburg Confession</u> 1:1–6, which specifically address those issues). The clause is often understood by Protestants to mean that the Spirit is sent from the Father, by the Son, a conception which is not controversial in either Catholicism or Eastern Orthodoxy. A representative view of Protestant Trinitarian theology is more difficult to provide, given the diverse and decentralized nature of the various Protestant churches.

Questions of logical coherency

Recently, there have been philosophical attempts to defend the logical coherency of Trinity, by <u>Richard Swinburne</u> and by <u>Peter Geach</u> et al. The formulation suggested by Swinburne is free from logical incoherency, but it is debatable whether this formulation is consistent with historical orthodoxy. Regarding the formulation suggested by Geach, not all philosophers would agree with its logical coherency. Swinburne has suggested that "the Father, the Son and the Holy Spirit be thought of as numerically distinct Gods". Geach suggested that "a coherent statement of the doctrine is possible on the assumption that identity is "always relative to a sortal term".

Some <u>Messianic</u> groups, the <u>Branch Davidian</u>, and even some scholars within (but not necessarily representing) denominations such as <u>Southern Baptist Convention</u> view the Trinity as being comparable to a family, hence the familial terms of Father, Son, and the implied role of Mother for the Holy Spirit. The Hebrew word for "God", *Elohim*, which has an inherent plurality, has the function as a surname as in *Yahweh Elohim*. The seeming contradiction of Elohim being "one" is solved by the fact that the Hebrew word for "one", *echad*, can describe a compound unity, harmonious in direction and purpose; unlike *yachid* which means singularity.

An argument against the logical coherency of an idea of the Trinity as composed of parts is the following: If God has compositional parts, they are either finite or infinite parts. If finite, then God is finite. If infinite, then there are multiple infinities. Each case becomes a denial of monotheism. The belief in compositional parts has therefore been regarded as a <u>heresy</u> since the establishment of the Nicene Creed, a condemnation reaffirmed in Protestant Creeds such as the <u>Westminster Confession of Faith</u> and <u>1689 Baptist Confession of Faith</u> which state "God has no parts." <u>Louis Berkhof</u> describes the doctrine of the Trinity requiring belief in a "simplex unity" and not a complex (or composite) being. "There is in the Divine Being but one indivisible essence" and "The whole undivided essence of God belongs equally to each of the three persons."

Eastern Orthodox tradition

Direct representations of the Trinity are much rarer in <u>Eastern Orthodox</u> art of any period—reservations about depicting the Father remain fairly strong, as they were in the West until the high Middle Ages. The <u>Second Council of Nicea</u> in 787 confirmed that the depiction of Christ was allowed because he became man; the situation regarding the Father was less clear. The usual <u>Orthodox representation</u> of the Trinity was through the "Old Testament Trinity" of the three angels visiting Abraham—said in the text to be "the Lord"[Genesis 18:1-15]. However scholars generally agree that the direct representation of the Trinity began in Greek works from the 11th century onwards, where Christ is shown as an infant sitting on the Father's lap, with the Dove of the Holy Spirit also present. Such depictions spread to the West and became the standard type there, though with an adult Christ, as described above. This type later spread back to the Orthodox world where <u>post-Byzantine</u> representations similar to those in the West are not uncommon outside Russia. The subject long remained sensitive, and the <u>Russian Orthodox Church</u> at the Great Synod of Moscow in 1667 finally forbade depictions of the Father in human form. The canon is quoted in full here because it explains the Russian Orthodox theology on the subject:

Chapter 2, §44: It is most absurd and improper to depict in <u>icons</u> the <u>Lord Sabaoth</u> (that is to say, <u>God the Father</u>) with a grey beard and the Only-Begotten Son in His bosom with a dove between them, because no-one has seen the Father according to His Divinity, and the Father has no flesh, nor was the Son born in the flesh from the Father before the ages. And though <u>David</u> the <u>prophet</u> says, "From the womb before the morning star have I begotten Thee"[Psalm 109:3], that birth was not fleshly, but unspeakable and incomprehensible. For Christ Himself says in the holy Gospel, "No man hath seen the Father, save the Son".[cf. [John 6:46]] And Isaiah the prophet says in his fortieth chapter: "To whom have ye likened the Lord? and with what likeness have ye made a similitude of Him? Has not the artificier of wood made an image, or the goldsmiths, having melted gold, gilt it over, and made it a similitude?"[Isa. 40:18-19] In like manner the Apostle Paul says in Acts[Acts 17:29] "Forasmuch then as we are the offspring of God, we ought not to think that the Godhead is like unto gold or silver or stone, graven by art of man's imagination." And John Damascene says: "But furthermore, who can make a similitude of the invisible, incorporeal, uncircumscribed and undepictable God? It is, then, uttermost insanity and impiety to give a form to the Godhead" (*Orthodox Faith*, 4:16). In like manner St. Gregory the Dialogist prohibits this. For this reason we should only form an understanding in the mind of Sabaoth, which is the Godhead, and of that birth before the ages of the Only-Begotten-Son from the Father, but we should never, in any wise depict these in icons, for this, indeed, is impossible. And the Holy Spirit is not in essence a dove, but in essence he is God, and "No man hath seen God", as John the Theologian and Evangelist bears witness[John 1:18] and this is so even though, at the Jordan at Christ's holy Baptism the Holy Spirit appeared in the likeness of a dove. For this reason, it is fitting on this occasion only to depict the Holy Spirit in the likeness of a dove. But in any other place those who have intelligence will not depict the Holy Spirit in the likeness of a dove. For on Mount Tabor, He appeared as a cloud and, at another time, in other ways. Furthermore, Sabaoth is the name not only of the Father, but of the Holy Trinity. According to Dionysios the Areopagite, Lord Sabaoth, translated from the Jewish tongue, means "Lord of Hosts". This Lord of Hosts is the Holy Trinity, Father, Son and Holy Spirit. And although Daniel the prophet says that he beheld the Ancient of Days sitting on a throne, this should not be understood to refer to the Father, but to the Son, Who at His second coming will judge every nation at the dreadful Judgment.

Ambivalence to Trinitarian doctrine

Some Protestant Christians, particularly some members of the restoration movement, are ambivalent about the doctrine of the Trinity. While not specifically rejecting Trinitarianism or presenting an alternative doctrine of the Godhead and God's relationship with humanity, they are neither dogmatic about the Trinity nor hold it as a test of true Christian faith. Some, like the Society of Friends (Quakers) and Christian Unitarians, may reject all doctrinal or creedal tests of true faith, though not necessarily reject Trinitarian language. Others with a distinctive understanding of "Scripture alone", like some members of the restorationist Churches of Christ, say that since the doctrine of the Trinity is not clearly articulated in the Bible, it cannot be required for salvation. Still others may look to church tradition and say that there has always been a Christian tradition that faithfully followed Jesus without such a doctrine.

Non-orthodox Trinitarianism

The Church of Jesus Christ of Latter-day Saints (Mormons) identify the Trinity (or Godhead) as the Father, the Son, and the Holy Ghost, but with a different intention than the Nicene faith. They regard these three as individual members of a heavenly triumvirate, completely united with one another in purpose—each member of the Godhead being a distinct being of physical form (God the Father, Jesus Christ) or spiritual form (The Holy Ghost.) Mormons draw their understanding of the Godhead primarily from the First Vision of Joseph Smith, Jr., who claimed to have seen God the Father and Jesus Christ and recounted seeing "two personages," one of which referred to the other as His "Beloved Son." Mormons also cite Biblical script to support their position that God the Father, Jesus Christ and the Holy Ghost are three distinct beings. *See* Matt 3, Mark 1, Luke 3, John 17, John 20:17, Acts 7:55-56. In this respect Mormon theology is more closely related to John Ascunages' early Tritheistic sect than to Orthodox Christianity. The primary author of this Monophysite group was John Philoponus.

He taught that there are three partial substances and one common substance in the trinity.

The Trinity in Christian Science is found in the unity of God, Christ, and the Holy Ghost or—"God the Father-Mother; Christ the spiritual idea of sonship; divine Science or the Holy Comforter." The same in essence, the Trinity indicates "the intelligent relation of God to man and the universe".

Nontrinitarianism

Some Christian traditions either reject the doctrine of the Trinity or consider it unimportant. Persons and groups espousing this position generally do not refer to themselves as "Nontrinitarians". They can vary in both their reasons for rejecting traditional teaching on the Trinity, and in the way they describe God.

Nontrinitarian groups

Since Trinitarianism is central to so much of church doctrine, nontrinitarians were mostly groups that existed before the Nicene Creed was codified in 325 or are groups that developed after the Reformation, when many church doctrines came into question. In the early centuries of Christian history Adoptionists, Arians, Ebionites, some Gnostics, Marcionites, and others held nontrinitarian beliefs. The Nicene Creed raised the issue of the relationship between Jesus' divine and human natures. Monophysitism ("one nature") and monothelitism ("one will") were early attempts, considered heretical by trinitarians, to explain this relationship.

During more than a thousand years of Trinitarian orthodoxy, formal nontrinitarianism, i.e., a doctrine held by a church, group, or movement, was rare, but it did appear. For example, among the Cathars of the 13th century. The Protestant Reformation of the 1500s also brought tradition into question. At first, nontrinitarians were executed (such as Servetus), or forced to keep their beliefs secret (such as Isaac

Newton). The eventual establishment of religious freedom, however, allowed nontrinitarians to more easily preach their beliefs, and the 19th century saw the establishment of several nontrinitarian groups in North America and elsewhere. These include Christadelphians, Jehovah's Witnesses, The Church of Jesus Christ of Latter-day Saints, and Unitarians. Servetus heavily influenced the theology of Emanuel Swedenborg; the church founded on his writings is a small but influential nontrinitarian movement. Some groups espousing Binitarianism such as the Living Church of God claim that Binitarianism was the majority view of those that professed Christ in the second century.

Twentieth-century nontrinitarian movements include Iglesia ni Cristo, Most Holy Church of God in Christ Jesus, and the Unification Church. Nontrinitarian groups differ from one another in their views of Jesus Christ, depicting him variously as a divine being second only to God the Father (e.g., Jehovah's Witnesses), as Yahweh of the Old Testament in human form, as God (but not eternally God), as Son of God but inferior to the Father (versus co-equal), as a prophet, or simply as a holy man.

Oneness Pentecostals deny traditional Trinitarian doctrine, while affirming their belief that God took on flesh in the man Jesus Christ. Like Trinitarians, Oneness adherents believe that Jesus Christ is fully God and fully man. However, whereas Trinitarians believe that "God the Son" (a being whose existence is denied in Oneness theology), the eternal second person of the Trinity, became man, Oneness adherents hold that the one and only true God—who manifests himself in any way he chooses, including as Father, Son and Holy Spirit—became man. Oneness believers view "Father", "Son" and "Holy Spirit" as *titles*, reflecting different manifestations of the one true God in the universe. Oneness Pentecostals are regarded by orthodox Christians as subscribing to the heresy of Modalism, teaching that God displayed himself in the Old Testament as Father, in the Gospels as the Son, and after the Ascension as the Holy Spirit, which is not the orthodox doctrine of three distinct and eternal Persons in one divine essence. Rather, Oneness teaches that there is only one being, revealing himself in different ways.

121

Bibliography

- Bigham, Steven, *Image of God the Father in Orthodox Theology and Iconography*, Studies in Orthodox iconography, St Vladimir's Seminary Press, 1995, ISBN 1879038153, 97818790381, Google books
- Paul Fiddes, *The Trinity in worship and preaching* (London: London Baptist Preachers' Association, 1991)
- Paul Fiddes, *Participating in God : a pastoral doctrine of the Trinity* (London: Darton, Longman, & Todd, 2000)
- Roger E. Olson, *The Story of Christian Theology : Twenty Centuries of Tradition & Reform* (Downers Grove: InterVarsity Press, 1999)
- William J. La Due, The Trinity guide to the Trinity (Continuum International Publishing Group, 2003 ISBN 1563383950, 9781563383953)

The Nicene Creed

We believe in one God,
the Father, the Almighty,
maker of heaven and earth
of all that is, seen and unseen.

We believe in one Lord, Jesus Christ,
the only Son of God,
eternally begotten of the Father,
God from God,
light from light
true God from true God,
begotten, not made,
of one Being with the Father,
through whom all things were made.
For us and for our salvation,
he came down from heaven:
by the power of the Holy Spirit
he became incarnate from the Virgin Mary,
and was made man.
For our sake he was crucified under Pontius Pilate;
He suffered death and was buried.
On the third day he rose again
in accordance with the scriptures;
he ascended into Heaven
and is seated at the right hand of the Father:
He shall come again to judge the living and the dead,
and his kingdom will have no end.

We believe in the Holy Spirit, the Lord, the giver of life,
who proceeds from the Father and the Son.
With the Father and the Son he is worshiped and glorified.
He has spoken through the prophets.

We believe in one holy catholic and apostolic church.

We acknowledge one baptism for the forgiveness of sins,
We look for the resurrection of our dead,
and the life of the world to come.
Amen.

Apostles Creed

1. I believe in God the Father, Almighty, Maker of heaven and earth:

2. And in Jesus Christ, his only begotten Son, our Lord:

3. Who was conceived by the Holy Ghost, born of the Virgin Mary:

4. Suffered under Pontius Pilate; was crucified, dead and buried: He descended into hell:

5. The third day he rose again from the dead:

6. He ascended into heaven, and sits at the right hand of God the Father Almighty:

7. From thence he shall come to judge the quick and the dead:

8. I believe in the Holy Ghost:

9. I believe in the holy catholic church: the communion of saints:

10. The forgiveness of sins:

11. The resurrection of the body:

12. And the life everlasting. Amen.

The Koran[13]

The Family of Imran

In the name of Allah, the Beneficent, the Merciful.

[**3.1**] Alif Lam Mim.

[**3.2**] Allah, (there is) no god but He, the Everliving, the Self-subsisting by Whom all things subsist

[**3.3**] He has revealed to you the Book with truth, verifying that which is before it, and He revealed the Tavrat and the Injeel aforetime, a guidance for the people, and He sent the Furqan.

[**3.4**] Surely they who disbelieve in the communications of Allah they shall have a severe chastisement; and Allah is Mighty, the Lord of retribution.

[**3.5**] Allah-- surely nothing is hidden from Him in the earth or in the heaven.

[**3.6**] He it is Who shapes you in the wombs as He likes; there is no god but He, the Mighty, the Wise

[**3.7**] He it is Who has revealed the Book to you; some of its verses are decisive, they are the basis of the Book, and others are allegorical; then as for those in whose hearts there is perversity they follow the part of it which is allegorical, seeking to mislead and seeking to give it (their own) interpretation. but none knows its interpretation except Allah, and those who are firmly rooted in knowledge say: We believe in it, it is all from our Lord; and none do mind except those having understanding.

[**3.8**] Our Lord! make not our hearts to deviate after Thou hast guided us aright, and grant us from Thee mercy; surely Thou art the most liberal Giver.

[**3.9**] Our Lord! surely Thou art the Gatherer of men on a day about which there is no doubt; surely Allah will not fail (His) promise.

---

[13] Online book initiative

[**3.10**] (As for) those who disbelieve, surely neither their wealth nor their children shall avail them in the least against Allah, and these it is who are the fuel of the fire.

[**3.11**] Like the striving of the people of Firon and those before them; they rejected Our communications, so Allah destroyed them on account of their faults; and Allah is severe in requiting (evil).

[**3.12**] Say to those who disbelieve: You shall be vanquished, and driven together to hell; and evil is the resting-place.

[**3.13**] Indeed there was a sign for you in the two hosts (which) met together in encounter; one party fighting in the way of Allah and the other unbelieving, whom they saw twice as.many as themselves with the sight of the eye and Allah strengthens with His aid whom He pleases; most surely there is a lesson in this for those who have sight.

[**3.14**] The love of desires, of women and sons and hoarded treasures of gold and silver and well bred horses and cattle and tilth, is made to seem fair to men; this is the provision of the life of this world; and Allah is He with Whom is the good goal (of life).

[**3.15**] Say:Shall I tell you what is better than these? For those who guard (against evil) are gardens with their Lord, beneath which rivers flow, to abide in them, and pure mates and Allah's pleasure; and Allah sees the servants.

[**3.16**] Those who say: Our Lord! surely we believe, therefore forgive us our faults and save us from the chastisement of the fire.

[**3.17**] The patient, and the truthful, and the obedient, and those who spend (benevolently) and those who ask forgiveness in the morning times.

[**3.18**] Allah bears witness that there is no god but He, and (so do) the angels and those possessed of knowledge, maintaining His creation with justice; there is no god but He, the Mighty, the Wise.

[**3.19**] Surely the (true) religion with Allah is Islam, and those to whom the Book had been given did not show opposition but after knowledge had come to them, out of envy among themselves; and whoever disbelieves in the communications of Allah then surely Allah is quick in reckoning.

[**3.20**] But if they dispute with you, say: I have submitted myself entirely to Allah and (so) every one who follows me; and say to those who have been given the Book and the unlearned people: Do you submit yourselves? So if they submit then indeed they follow the right way; and if they turn back, then upon you is only the delivery of the message and Allah sees the servants.

[**3.21**] Surely (as for) those who disbelieve in the communications of Allah and slay the prophets unjustly and slay those among men who enjoin justice, announce to them a painful chastisement.

[**3.22**] Those are they whose works shall become null in this world as well as the hereafter, and they shall have no helpers.

[**3.23**] Have you not considered those (Jews) who are given a portion of the Book? They are invited to the Book of Allah that it might decide between them, then a part of them turn back and they withdraw.

[**3.24**] This is because they say: The fire shall not touch us but for a few days; and what they have forged deceives them in the matter of their religion.

[**3.25**] Then how will it be when We shall gather them together on a day about which there is no doubt, and every soul shall be fully paid what it has earned, and they shall not be dealt with unjustly?

[**3.26**] Say: O Allah, Master of the Kingdom! Thou givest the kingdom to whomsoever Thou pleasest and takest away the kingdom from whomsoever Thou pleasest, and Thou exaltest whom Thou pleasest and abasest whom Thou pleasest in Thine hand is the good; surety, Thou hast power over all things.

[**3.27**] Thou makest the night to pass into the day and Thou makest the day to pass into the night, and Thou bringest forth the living from the dead and Thou bringest forth the dead from the living, and Thou givest sustenance to whom Thou pleasest without measure.

[**3.28**] Let not the believers take the unbelievers for friends rather than believers; and whoever does this, he shall have nothing of (the guardianship of) Allah, but you should guard yourselves against them, guarding carefully; and Allah makes you cautious of (retribution from) Himself; and to Allah is the eventual coming.

[**3.29**] Say: Whether you hide what is in your hearts or manifest it, Allah knows it, and He knows whatever is in the heavens and whatever is in the earth, and Allah has power over all things.

[**3.30**] On the day that every soul shall find present what it has done of good and what it has done of evil, it shall wish that between it and that (evil) there were a long duration of time; and Allah makes you to be cautious of (retribution from) Himself; and Allah is Compassionate to the servants.

[**3.31**] Say: If you love Allah, then follow me, Allah will love you and forgive you your faults, and Allah is Forgiving, MercifuL

[**3.32**] Say: Obey Allah and the Apostle; but if they turn back, then surely Allah does not love the unbelievers.

[**3.33**] Surely Allah chose Adam and Nuh and the descendants of Ibrahim and the descendants of Imran above the nations.

[**3.34**] Offspring one of the other; and Allah is Hearing, Knowing.

[**3.35**] When a woman of Imran said: My Lord! surely I vow to Thee what is in my womb, to be devoted (to Thy service); accept therefore from me, surely Thou art the Hearing, the Knowing.

[**3.36**] So when she brought forth, she said: My Lord! Surely I have brought it forth a female-- and Allah knew best what she brought forth-- and the male is not like the female, and I have named it Marium, and I commend her and her offspring into Thy protection from the accursed Shaitan.

[**3.37**] So her Lord accepted her with a good acceptance and made her grow up a good growing, and gave her into the charge of Zakariya; whenever Zakariya entered the sanctuary to (see) her, he found with her food. He said: O Marium! whence comes this to you? She said: It is from Allah. Surely Allah gives to whom He pleases without measure.

[**3.38**] There did Zakariya pray to his Lord; he said: My Lord! grant me from Thee good offspring; surely Thou art the Hearer of prayer.

[**3.39**] Then the angels called to him as he stood praying in the sanctuary: That Allah gives you the good news of Yahya verifying a Word from Allah, and honorable and chaste and a prophet from among the good ones.

[**3.40**] He said: My Lord! when shall there be a son (born) to me, and old age has already come upon me, and my wife is barren? He said: even thus does Allah what He pleases.

[**3.41**] He said: My Lord! appoint a sign for me. Said He: Your sign is that you should not speak to men for three days except by signs; and remember your Lord much and glorify Him in the evening and the morning. f42. And when the angels said: O Marium! surely Allah has chosen you and purified you and chosen you above the women of of the world.

[**3.43**] O Marium! keep to obedience to your Lord and humble yourself, and bow down with those who bow.

[**3.44**] This is of the announcements relating to the unseen which We reveal to you; and you were not with them when they cast their pens (to decide) which of them should have Marium in his charge, and you were not with them when they contended one with another.

[**3.45**] **When the angels said: O Marium, surely Allah gives you good news with a Word from Him (of one) whose name is the '. Messiah, Isa (Jesus)*son of Marium, worthy of regard in this world and the hereafter and of those who are made near (to Allah).**

[**3.46**] **And he shall speak to the people when in the cradle and when of old age, and (he shall be) one of the good ones.**

[**3.47**] **She said: My Lord! when shall there be a son (born) to I me, and man has not touched me? He said: Even so, Allah creates what He pleases; when He has decreed a matter, He only says to it, Be, and it is.**

[**3.48**] **And He will teach him the Book and the wisdom and the Tavrat and the Injeel.**

[**3.49**] **And (make him) an apostle to the children of Israel: That I have come to you with a sign from your Lord, that I determine for you out of dust like the form of a bird, then I breathe into it and it becomes a bird with Allah's permission and I heal the blind and the leprous, and bring the dead to life with Allah's permission and I inform you of what you should eat and what you should store in your houses; most surely there is a sign in this for you, if you are believers.**

[**3.50**] And a verifier of that which is before me of the Taurat and that I may allow you part of that which has been forbidden t you, and I have come to you with a sign from your Lord therefore be careful of (your duty to) Allah and obey me.

[**3.51**] Surely Allah is my Lord and your Lord, therefore serve Him; this is the right path.

[**3.52**] But when Isa perceived unbelief on their part, he said Who will be my helpers in Allah's way? The disciples said: We are helpers (in the way) of Allah: We believe in Allah and bear witness that we are submitting ones.

[**3.53**] Our Lord! we believe in what Thou hast revealed and we follow the apostle, so write us down with those who bear witness.

[**3.54**] And they planned and Allah (also) planned, and Allah is the best of planners.

[**3.55**] And when Allah said: O Isa, I am going to terminate the period of your stay (on earth) and cause you to ascend unto Me and purify you of those who disbelieve and make those who follow you above those who disbelieve to the day of resurrection; then to Me shall be your return, so l will decide between you concerning that in which you differed.

[**3.56**] Then as to those who disbelieve, I will chastise them with severe chastisement in this world and the hereafter, and they shall have no helpers.

[**3.57**] And as to those who believe and do good deeds, He will pay them fully their rewards; and Allah does not love the unjust.

[**3.58**] This We recite to you of the communications and the wise reminder.

[**3.59**] Surely the likeness of Isa is with Allah as the likeness of Adam; He created him from dust, then said to him, Be, and he was.

[**3.60**] (This is) the truth from your Lord, so be not of the disputers.

[**3.61**] But whoever disputes with you in this matter after what has come to you of knowledge, then say: Come let us call our sons and your sons and our women and your women and our near people and your near people, then let us be earnest in prayer, and pray for the curse of Allah on the liars.

[**3.62**] Most surely this is the true explanation, and there is no god but Allah; and most surely Allah-- He is the Mighty, the Wise.

[**3.63**] But if they turn back, then surely Allah knows the mischief-makers.

[**3.64**] Say: O followers of the Book! come to an equitable proposition between us and you that we shall not serve any but Allah and (that) we shall not associate aught with Him, and (that) some of us shall not take others for lords besides Allah; but if they turn back, then say: Bear witness that we are Muslims.

[**3.65**] O followers of the Book! why do you dispute about Ibrahim, when the Taurat and the Injeel were not revealed till after him; do you not then understand?

[**3.66**] Behold! you are they who disputed about that of which you had knowledge; why then do you dispute about that of which you have no knowledge? And Allah knows while you do not know.

[**3.67**] Ibrahim was not a Jew nor a Christian but he was (an) upright (man), a Muslim, and he was not one of the polytheists.

[**3.68**] Most surely the nearest of people to Ibrahim are those who followed him and this Prophet and those who believe and Allah is the guardian of the believers.

[**3.69**] A party of the followers of the Book desire that they should lead you astray, and they lead not astray but themselves, and they do not perceive.

[**3.70**] O followers of the Book! Why do you disbelieve in the communications of Allah while you witness (them)?

[**3.71**] O followers of the Book! Why do you confound the truth with the falsehood and hide the truth while you know?

[**3.72**] And a party of the followers of the Book say: Avow belief in that which has been revealed to those who believe, in the first part of the day, and disbelieve at the end of it, perhaps they go back on their religion.

[**3.73**] And do not believe but in him who follows your religion. Say: Surely the (true) guidance is the guidance of Allah-- that one may be given (by Him) the like of what you were given; or they would contend with you by an argument before your Lord. Say: Surely grace is in the hand of Allah, He gives it to whom He pleases; and Allah is Ample-giving, Knowing.

[**3.74**] He specially chooses for His mercy whom He pleases; and Allah is the Lord of mighty grace.

[**3.75**] And among the followers of the Book there are some such that if you entrust one (of them) with a heap of wealth, he shall pay it back to you; and among them there are some such that if you entrust one (of them) with a dinar he shall not pay it back to you except so long as you remain firm in demanding it; this is because they say: There is not upon us in the matter of the unlearned people any way (to reproach); and they tell a lie against Allah while they know.

[**3.76**] Yea, whoever fulfills his promise and guards (against evil)-- then surely Allah loves those who guard (against evil).

[**3.77**] (As for) those who take a small price for the covenant of Allah and their own oaths-- surely they shall have no portion in the hereafter, and Allah will not speak to them, nor will He look upon them on the day of resurrection nor will He purify them, and they shall have a painful chastisement.

[**3.78**] Most surely there is a party amongst those who distort the Book with their tongue that you may consider it to be (a part) of the Book, and they say, It is from Allah, while it is not from Allah, and they tell a lie against Allah whilst they know.

[**3.79**] It is not meet for a mortal that Allah should give him the Book and the wisdom and prophethood, then he should say to men: Be my servants rather than Allah's; but rather (he would say): Be worshippers of the Lord because of your teaching the Book and your reading (it yourselves).

[**3.80**] And neither would he enjoin you that you should take the angels and the prophets for lords; what! would he enjoin you with unbelief after you are Muslims?

[**3.81**] And when Allah made a covenant through the prophets: Certainly what I have given you of Book and wisdom-- then an apostle comes to you verifying that which is with you, you must believe in him, and you must aid him. He said: Do you affirm and accept My compact in this (matter)? They said: We do affirm. He said: Then bear witness, and I (too) am of the bearers of witness with you.

[**3.82**] Whoever therefore turns back after this, these it is that are the transgressors.

[3.83] Is it then other than Allah's religion that they seek (to follow), and to Him submits whoever is in the heavens and the earth, willingly or unwillingly, and to Him shall they be returned.

[3.84] Say: We believe in Allah and what has been revealed to us, and what was revealed to Ibrahim and Ismail and Ishaq and Yaqoub and the tribes, and what was given to Musa and Isa and to the prophets from their Lord; we do not make any distinction between any of them, and to Him do we submit.

[3.85] And whoever desires a religion other than Islam, it shall not be accepted from him, and in the hereafter he shall be one of the losers.

[3.86] How shall Allah guide a people who disbelieved after their believing and (after) they had borne witness that the Apostle was true and clear arguments had come to them; and Allah does not guide the unjust people.

[3.87] (As for) these, their reward is that upon them is the curse of Allah and the angels and of men, all together.

[3.88] Abiding in it; their chastisement shall not be lightened nor shall they be respited.

[3.89] Except those who repent after that and amend, then surely Allah is Forgiving, Merciful.

[3.90] Surely, those who disbelieve a,fter their believing, then increase in unbelief, their repentance shall not be accepted, and these are they that go astray.

[3.91] Surely, those who disbelieve and die while they are unbelievers, the earth full of gold shall not be accepted from one of them, though he should offer to ransom himself with it, these it is who shall have a painful chastisement, and they shall have no helpers.

[3.92] By no means shall you attain to righteousness until you spend (benevolently) out of what you love; and whatever thing you spend, Allah surely knows it.

[3.93] All food was lawful to the children of Israel except that which Israel had forbidden to himself, before the Taurat was revealed. Say: Bring then the Taurat and read it, if you are truthful.

[3.94] Then whoever fabricates a lie against Allah after this, these it is that are the unjust.

134

[**3.95**] Say: Allah has spoken the truth, therefore follow the religion of Ibrahim, the upright one; and he was not one of the polytheists.

[**3.96**] Most surely the first house appointed for men is the one at Bekka, blessed and a guidance for the nations.

[**3.**97] In it are clear signs, the standing place of Ibrahim, and whoever enters it shall be secure, and pilgrimage to the House is incumbent upon men for the sake of Allah, (upon) every one who is able to undertake the journey to it; and whoever disbelieves, then surely Allah is Self-sufficient, above any need of the worlds.

[**3.98**] Say: O followers of the Book! why do you disbelieve in the communications of Allah? And Allah is a witness of what you do.

[**3.99**] Say: O followers of the Book! why do you hinder him who believes from the way of Allah? You seek (to make) it crooked, while you are witness, and Allah is not heedless of what you do.

[**3.100**] O you who believe! if you obey a party from among those who have been given the Book, they will turn you back as unbelievers after you have believed.

[**3.101**] But how can you disbelieve while it is you to whom the communications of Allah are recited, and among you is His Apostle? And whoever holds fast to Allah, he indeed is guided to the right path.

[**3.102**] O you who believe! be careful of (your duty to) Allah with the care which is due to Him, and do not die unless you are Muslims.

[**3.103**] And hold fast by the covenant of Allah all together and be not disunited, and remember the favor of Allah on you when you were enemies, then He united your hearts so by His favor you became brethren; and you were on the brink of a pit of fire, then He saved you from it, thus does Allah make clear to you His communications that you may follow the right way.

[**3.104**] And from among you there should be a party who invite to good and enjoin what is right and forbid the wrong, and these it is that shall be successful.

[**3.105**] And be not like those who became divided and disagreed after clear arguments had come to them, and these it is that shall have a grievous chastisement.

[**3.106**] On the day when (some) faces shall turn white and (some) faces shall turn black; then as to those whose faces turn black: Did you disbelieve after your believing? Taste therefore the chastisement because you disbelieved.

[**3.107**] And as to those whose faces turn white, they shall be in Allah's mercy; in it they shall-abide.

[**3.108**] These are the communications of Allah which We recite to you with truth, and Allah does not desire any injustice to the creatures.

[**3.109**] And whatever is in the heavens and whatever is in the earth is Allah's; and to Allah all things return

[**3.110**] You are the best of the nations raised up for (the benefit of) men; you enjoin what is right and forbid the wrong and believe in Allah; and if the followers of the Book had believed it would have been better for them; of them (some) are believers and most of them are transgressors.

[**3.111**] They shall by no means harm you but with a slight evil; and if they fight with you they shall turn (their) backs to you, then shall they not be helped.

[**3.112**] Abasement is made to cleave to them wherever they are found, except under a covenant with Allah and a covenant with men, and they have become deserving of wrath from Allah, and humiliation is made to cleave to them; this is because they disbelieved in the communications of Allah and slew the prophets unjustly; this is because they disobeyed and exceeded the limits.

[**3.113**] They are not all alike; of the followers of the Book there is an upright party; they recite Allah's communications in the nighttime and they adore (Him).

[**3.114**] They believe in Allah and the last day, and they enjoin what is right and forbid the wrong and they strive with one another in hastening to good deeds, and those are among the good.

[**3.115**] And whatever good they do, they shall not be denied it, and Allah knows those who guard (against evil).

[**3.116**] (As for) those who disbelieve, surely neither their wealth nor their children shall avail them in the least against Allah; and these are the inmates of the fire; therein they shall abide.

[**3.117**] The likeness of what they spend in the life of this world is as the likeness of wind in which is intense cold (that) smites the seed produce of a people who haw done injustice to their souls and destroys it; and Allah is not unjust to them, but they are unjust to themselves. [**3.118**] O you who believe! do not take for intimate friends from among others than your own people; they do not fall short of inflicting loss upon you; they love what distresses you; vehement hatred has already appeared from out of their mouths, and what their breasts conceal is greater still; indeed, We have made the communications clear to you, if you will understand.

[**3.119**] Lo! you are they who will love them while they do not love you, and you believe in the Book (in) the whole of it; and when they meet you they say: We believe, and when they are alone, they bite the ends of their fingers in rage against you. Say: Die in your rage; surely Allah knows what is in the breasts.

[**3.120**] If good befalls you, it grieves them, and if an evil afflicts you, they rejoice at it; and if you are patient and guard yourselves, their scheme will not injure you in any way; surely Allah comprehends what they do.

[**3.121**] And when you did go forth early in the morning from your family to lodge the believers in encampments for war and Allah is Hearing, Knowing.

[**3.122**] When two parties from among you had determined that they should show cowardice, and Allah was the guardian of them both, and in Allah should the believers trust.

[**3.123**] And Allah did certainly assist you at Badr when you were weak; be careful of (your duty to) Allah then, that you may give thanks.

[**3.124**] When you said to the believers: Does it not suffice you that your Lord should assist you with three thousand of the angels sent down?

[**3.125**] Yea! if you remain patient and are on your guard, and they come upon you in a headlong manner, your Lord will assist you with five thousand of the havoc-making angels.

[**3.126**] And Allah did not make it but as good news for you, and that your hearts might be at ease thereby, and victory is only from Allah, the Mighty, the Wise.

[**3.127**] That He may cut off a portion from among those who disbelieve, or abase them so that they should return disappointed of attaining what they desired.

[**3.128**] You have no concern in the affair whether He turns to them (mercifully) or chastises them, for surely they are unjust.

[**3.129**] And whatever is in the heavens and whatever is in the earth is Allah's; He forgives whom He pleases and chastises whom He pleases; and Allah is Forgiving, Merciful.

[**3.130**] O you who believe! do not devour usury, making it double and redouble, and be careful of (your duty to) Allah, that you may be successful.

[**3.131**] And guard yourselves against the fire which has been prepared for the unbelievers.

[**3.132**] And obey Allah and the Apostle, that you may be shown mercy.

[**3.133**] And hasten to forgiveness from your Lord; and a Garden, the extensiveness of which is (as) the heavens and the earth, it is prepared for those who guard (against evil).

[**3.134**] Those who spend (benevolently) in ease as well as in straitness, and those who restrain (their) anger and pardon men; and Allah loves the doers of good (to others).

[**3.135**] And those who when they commit an indecency or do injustice to their souls remember Allah and ask forgiveness for their faults-- and who forgives the faults but Allah, and (who) do not knowingly persist in what they have done.

[**3.136**] (As for) these-- their reward is forgiveness from their Lord, and gardens beneath which rivers flow, to abide in them, and excellent is the reward of the laborers.

[**3.137**] Indeed there have been examples before you; therefore travel in the earth and see what was the end of the rejecters.

[**3.138**] This is a clear statement for men, and a guidance and an admonition to those who guard (against evil).

[**3.139**] And be not infirm, and be not grieving, and you shall have the upper hand if you are believers.

[**3.140**] If a wound has afflicted you (at Ohud), a wound like it has also afflicted the (unbelieving) people; and We bring these days to men by turns, and that Allah may know those who believe and take witnesses from among you; and Allah does not love the unjust.

[**3.141**] And that He may purge those who believe and deprive the unbelievers of blessings.

[**3.142**] Do you think that you will enter the garden while Allah has not yet known those who strive hard from among you, and (He has not) known the patient.

[**3.143**] And certainly you desired death before you met it, so indeed you have seen it and you look (at it)

[**3.144**] And Muhammad is no more than an apostle; the apostles have already passed away before him; if then he dies or is killed will you turn back upon your heels? And whoever turns back upon his heels!s, he will by no means do harm to Allah in the least and Allah will reward the grateful.

[**3.145**] And a soul will not die but with the permission of Allah the term is fixed; and whoever desires the reward of this world, I shall give him of it, and whoever desires the reward of the hereafter I shall give him of it, and I will reward the grateful.

[**3.146**] And how many a prophet has fought with whom were many worshippers of the Lord; so they did not become weak-hearted on account of what befell them in Allah's way, nor did they weaken, nor did they abase themselves; and Allah loves the patient.

[**3.147**] And their saying was no other than that they said: Our Lord! forgive us our faults and our extravagance in our affair and make firm our feet and help us against the unbelieving people.

[**3.148**] So Allah gave them the reward of this world and better reward of the hereafter and Allah loves those who do good (to others).

[**3.149**] O you who believe! if you obey those who disbelieve they will turn you back upon your heels, so you will turn back losers.

[**3.150**] Nay! Allah is your Patron and He is the best of the helpers.

[**3.151**] We will cast terror into the hearts of those who disbelieve, because they set up with Allah that for which He has sent down no authority, and their abode is the fire, and evil is the abode of the unjust.

[**3.152**] And certainly Allah made good to you His promise when you slew them by His permission, until when you became weak-hearted and disputed about the affair and disobeyed after He had shown you that which you loved; of you were some who desired this world and of you were some who desired the hereafter; then He turned you away from them that He might try you; and He has certainly pardoned you, and Allah is Gracious to the believers.

[**3.153**] When you ran off precipitately and did not wait for any one, and the Apostle was calling you from your rear, so He gave you another sorrow instead of (your) sorrow, so that you might not grieve at what had escaped you, nor (at) what befell you; and Allah is aware of what you do.

[**3.154**] Then after sorrow He sent down security upon you, a calm coming upon a party of you, and (there was) another party whom their own souls had rendered anxious; they entertained about Allah thoughts of ignorance quite unjustly, saying: We have no hand in the affair. Say: Surely the affair is wholly (in the hands) of Allah. They conceal within their souls what they would not reveal to you. They say: Had we any hand in the affair, we would not have been slain here. Say: Had you remained in your houses, those for whom slaughter was ordained would certainly have gone forth to the places where they would be slain, and that Allah might test what was in your breasts and that He might purge what was in your hearts; and Allah knows what is in the breasts.

[**3.155**] (As for) those of you who turned back on the day when the two armies met, only the Shaitan sought to cause them to make a slip on account of some deeds they had done, and certainly Allah has pardoned them; surely Allah is Forgiving, Forbearing.

[**3.156**] O you who believe! be not like those who disbelieve and say of their brethren when they travel in the earth or engage in fighting: Had they been with us, they would not have died and they would not have been slain; so Allah makes this to be an intense regret in their hearts; and Allah gives life and causes death and Allah sees what you do.

[**3.157**] And if you are slain in the way of Allah or you die, certainly forgiveness from Allah and mercy is better than what they amass.

[**3.158**] And if indeed you die or you are slain, certainly to Allah shall you be gathered together.

[**3.159**] Thus it is due to mercy from Allah that you deal with them gently, and had you been rough, hard hearted, they would certainly have dispersed from around you; pardon them therefore and ask pardon for them, and take counsel with them in the affair; so when you have decided, then place your trust in Allah; surely Allah loves those who trust.

[**3.160**] If Allah assists you, then there is none that can overcome you, and if He forsakes you, who is there then that can assist you after Him? And on Allah should the believers rely.

[**3.161**] And it is not attributable to a prophet that he should act unfaithfully; and he who acts unfaithfully shall bring that in respect of which he has acted unfaithfully on the day of resurrection; then shall every soul be paid back fully what it has earned, and they shall not be dealt with unjustly.

[**3.162**] Is then he who follows the pleasure of Allah like him who has made himself deserving of displeasure from Allah, and his abode is hell; and it is an evil destination.

[**3.163**] There are (varying) grades with Allah, and Allah sees what they do.

[**3.164**] Certainly Allah conferred a benefit upon the believers when He raised among them an Apostle from among themselves, reciting to them His communications and purifying them, and teaching them the Book and the wisdom, although before that they were surely in manifest error.

[**3.165**] What! when a misfortune befell you, and you had certainly afflicted (the unbelievers) with twice as much, you began to say: Whence is this? Say: It is from yourselves; surely Allah has power over all things.

[**3.166**] And what befell you on the day when the two armies met (at Ohud) was with Allah's knowledge, and that He might know the believers.

[**3.167**] And that He might know the hypocrites; and it was said to them: Come, fight in Allah's way, or defend yourselves. They said: If we knew fighting, we would certainly have followed you. They were on that day much nearer to unbelief than to belief. They say with their mouths what is not in their hearts, and Allah best knows what they conceal.

[**3.168**] Those who said of their brethren whilst they (themselves) held back: Had they obeyed us, they would not have been killed. Say: Then avert death from yourselves if you speak the truth.

[**3.169**] And reckon not those who are killed in Allah's way as dead; nay, they are alive (and) are provided sustenance from their Lord;

[**3.170**] Rejoicing in what Allah has given them out of His grace and they rejoice for the sake of those who, (being left) behind them, have not yet joined them, that they shall have no fear, nor shall they grieve.

[**3.171**] They rejoice on account of favor from Allah and (His) grace, and that Allah will not waste the reward of the believers.

[**3.172**] (As for) those who responded (at Ohud) to the call of Allah and the Apostle after the wound had befallen them, those among them who do good (to others) and guard (against evil)shall have a great reward.

[**3.173**] Those to whom the people said: Surely men have gathered against you, therefore fear them, but this increased their faith, and they said: Allah is sufficient for us and most excellent is the Protector.

[**3.174**] So they returned with favor from Allah and (His) grace, no evil touched them and they followed the pleasure of Allah; and Allah is the Lord of mighty grace.

[**3.175**] It is only the Shaitan that causes you to fear from his friends, but do not fear them, and fear Me if you are believers.

[**3.176**] And let not those grieve you who fall into unbelief hastily; surely they can do no harm to Allah at all; Allah intends that He should not give them any portion in the hereafter, and they shall have a grievous chastisement.

[**3.177**] Surely those who have bought unbelief at the price of faith shall do no harm at all to Allah, and they shall have a painful chastisement.

[**3.178**] And let not those who disbelieve think that Our granting them respite is better for their souls; We grant them respite only that they may add to their sins; and they shall have a disgraceful chastisement.

[**3.179**] On no account will Allah leave the believers in the condition which you are in until He separates the evil from the good; nor is Allah going to make you acquainted with the unseen, but Allah chooses of

His apostles whom He pleases; therefore believe in Allah and His apostles; and if you believe and guard (against evil), then you shall have a great reward.

[**3.180**] And let not those deem, who are niggardly in giving away that which Allah has granted them out of His grace, that it is good for them; nay, it is worse for them; they shall have that whereof they were niggardly made to cleave to their necks on the resurrection day; and Allah's is the heritage of the heavens and the earth; and Allah is aware of what you do.

[**3.181**] Allah has certainly heard the saying of those who said: Surely Allah is poor and we are rich. I will record what they say, and their killing the prophets unjustly, and I will say: Taste the chastisement of burning.

[**3.182**] This is for what your own hands have sent before and because Allah is not in the least unjust to the servants.

[**3.183**] (Those are they) who said: Surely Allah has enjoined us that we should not believe in any apostle until he brings us an offering which the fire consumes. Say: Indeed, there came to you apostles before me with clear arguments and with that which you demand; why then did you kill them if you are truthful?

[**3.184**] But if they reject you, so indeed were rejected before you apostles who came with clear arguments and scriptures and the illuminating book.

[**3.185**] Every soul shall taste of death, and you shall only be paid fully your reward on the resurrection day; then whoever is removed far away from the fire and is made to enter the garden he indeed has attained the object; and the life of this world is nothing but a provision of vanities.

[**3.186**] You shall certainly be tried respecting your wealth and your souls, and you shall certainly hear from those who have been given the Book before you and from those who are polytheists much annoying talk; and if you are patient and guard (against evil), surely this is one of the affairs (which should be) determined upon.

[**3.187**] And when Allah made a covenant with those who were given the Book: You shall certainly make it known to men and you shall not hide it; but they cast it behind their backs and took a small price for it;

so evil is that which they buy.

[**3.188**] Do not think those who rejoice for what they have done and love that they should be praised for what they have not done-- so do by no means think them to be safe from the chastisement, and they shall have a painful chastisement.

[**3.189**] And Allah's is the kingdom of the heavens and the earth, and Allah has power over all things.

[**3.190**] Most surely in the creation of the heavens and the earth and the alternation of the night and the day there are signs for men who understand.

[**3.191**] Those who remember Allah standing and sitting and lying on their sides and reflect on the creation of the heavens and the earth: Our Lord! Thou hast not created this in vain! Glory be to Thee; save us then from the chastisement of the fire:

[**3.192**] Our Lord! surely whomsoever Thou makest enter the fire, him Thou hast indeed brought to disgrace, and there shall be no helpers for the unjust:

[**3.193**] Our Lord! surely we have heard a preacher calling to the faith, saying: Believe in your Lord, so we did believe; Our Lord! forgive us therefore our faults, and cover our evil deeds and make us die with the righteous.

[**3.194**] Our Lord! and grant us what Thou hast promised us by Thy apostles; and disgrace us not on the day of resurrection; surely Thou dost not fail to perform the promise.

[**3.195**] So their Lord accepted their prayer: That I will not waste the work of a worker among you, whether male or female, the one of you being from the other; they, therefore, who fled and were turned out of their homes and persecuted in My way and who fought and were slain, I will most certainly cover their evil deeds, and I will most certainly make them enter gardens beneath which rivers flow; a reward from Allah, and with Allah is yet better reward.

[**3.196**] Let it not deceive you that those who disbelieve go to and fro in the cities fearlessly.

[**3.197**] A brief enjoyment! then their abode is hell, and evil is the resting-place.

[**3.198**] But as to those who are careful of (their duty to) their Lord, they shall have gardens beneath which rivers flow, abiding in them; an entertainment from their Lord, and that which is with Allah is best for the righteous.

[**3.199**] And most surely of the followers of the Book there are those who believe in Allah and (in) that which has been revealed to you and (in) that which has been revealed to them, being lowly before Allah; they do not take a small price for the communications of Allah; these it is that have their reward with their Lord; surely Allah is quick in reckoning.

[**3.200**] O you who believe! be patient and excel in patience and remain steadfast, and be careful of (your duty to) Allah, that you may be successful.

*Added references, Isa = Jesus, Marium = Mary, Musa = Moses.

Monotheism

Monotheism (from Greek μόνος) is the belief in theology that only one diety exists.[1] The concept of "monotheism" tends to be dominated by the concept of God in the Abrahamic religions, such as Judaism, Christianity, Islam and Druze, the Platonic concept of God as put forward by Pseudo-Dionysius the Areopagite, as well as the Advaita, Dvaita and Vishishtadvaita philosophies of Hinduism, although the latter philosophies admit the existence of a plethora of divine beings including less-powerful deities such as devas.[2] Sikhism on the other hand, is a monotheistic Indian religion, in contrast to many schools of Hinduism and the other Indian religions.

Due to its Abrahamic association, the concept of monotheism has often been defined in contrast to polytheistic and pantheistic religions, and monotheism tends to overlap with other unitary concepts, such as monism.

Ostensibly monotheistic religions may still include concepts of a plurality of the divine. For example, the Trinity in which God is one being in three eternal persons (the Father, the Son and the Holy Spirit). Additionally, most Christian churches teach Jesus to be two natures (divine and human), each possessing the full attributes of that nature, without mixture or intermingling of those attributes. This view is not shared by all Christians, notably the Oriental Orthodox (miaphysite) churches.

Catholics venerate the saints, (among them Mary), as human beings who had remarkable qualities, lived their faith in God to the extreme and are believed to be capable of interceding in the process of salvation for others. The concept of monotheism in Islam and Judaism however, is far more direct, God's oneness being understood as absolutely unquestionable.

Origin and development

The word *monotheism* is derived from the Greek μόνος (*monos*) meaning "single" and θεός (*theos*) meaning "God". The English term was first used by Henry More (1614–1687).

The concept sees a gradual development out of notions of henotheism (worshiping a single god while accepting the existence or possible existence of other deities) and monolatrism (the recognition of the existence of many gods, but with the consistent worship of only one deity). In the ancient Near East, each city had a local patron deity, such as Shamash at Larsa or Sin at Ur. The first claims of global supremacy of a specific god date to the Late Bronze Age, with Akhenaten's *Great Hymn to the Aten* (speculatively connected to Judaism by Sigmund Freud in his *Moses and Monotheism*). Currents of monism or monotheism emerge in Vedic India in the same period, with e.g. the Nasadiya Sukta. Philosophical monotheism and the associated concept of absolute good and evil emerges in Judaism, later culminating in the doctrines of Christology in early Christianity and finally (by the 7th century) in the *tawhid* in Islam.

- Pantheism holds that the universe itself is God. The existence of a transcendent supreme extraneous to nature is denied.

Panentheism, is a form of monistic monotheism which holds that God is all of existence, Austrian anthropologist Wilhelm Schmidt in the 1910s postulated an *Urmonotheismus*, "original" or "primitive monotheism."

Historically, some ancient Near Eastern religions from the Late Bronze Age begin to exhibit aspects of monotheism or monolatrism.

This is notably the case with the Aten cult in the reign of the Egyptian pharaoh Akhenaten, but also with the rise of Marduk from the tutelary of Babylon to the claim of universal supremacy.

In Zoroastrianism, Ahura Mazda appears as a supreme and transcendental deity. Depending on the date of Zoroaster (usually placed in the early Iron Age), this may be one of the earliest documented instances of the emergence of monism in an Indo-European religion. Also in Indo-Iranian tradition, the Rigveda exhibits notions of monism, in particular in the comparatively late tenth book, also dated to the early Iron Age, e.g. in the Nasadiya sukta.

Varieties

Further information: Comparative religion, Conceptions of God, *and* Theism

Some argue that there are various forms of monotheism, including:

- Henotheism involves devotion to a single god while accepting the existence of other gods. Similarly, monolatrism is the worship of a single deity independent of the ontological claims regarding that deity.
- Deism posits the existence of a single god, or the Designer of the designs in Nature. Some Deists believe in an impersonal god that does not intervene in the world while other Deists believe in intervention through Providence.
- Monistic Theism is the type of monotheism found in Hinduism, encompassing pantheistic and panentheistic monism, and at the same time the concept of a personal god.
- containing, but not identical to, the Universe. The 'one God' is omnipotent and all-pervading, the universe is part of God, and God is both immanent and transcendent.
- Substance monotheism, found in some indigenous African religions, holds that the many gods are different forms of a single underlying substance.
- Trinitarian monotheism is the Christian doctrine of belief in one God who is three distinct persons; God the Father, God the Son & God the Holy Spirit.

On the surface, monotheism is in contrast with polytheism, which is the belief in several deities. Polytheism is however reconcilable with Inclusive monotheism, which claims that all deities are just different names or forms of a single god. This approach is common in Hinduism, e.g., in Smartism. Exclusive monotheism, on the other hand, actively opposes polytheism. Monotheism is often contrasted with theistic dualism (ditheism). However, in dualistic theologies as that of Gnosticism, the two deities are not of equal rank, and the role of the Gnostic demiurge is closer to that of Satan in Christian theology than that of a diarch on equal terms with God (who is represented in pantheistic fashion, as Pleroma).

Abrahamic religions

Further information: Abrahamic religion

The major source of monotheism in the modern Western World is the narrative of the Hebrew Bible, the source of Judaism. Judaism may have received influences from various non-biblical religions present in Egypt and Syria. This can be seen by the Torah's reference to Egyptian culture in Genesis and the story of Moses, as well as the mention of Hittite and Hurrian cultures of Syria in the Genesis story of Abraham. Although, orthodox Jews would dispute this based on the Jewish fundamental that the Torah was received from God on Mount Sinai in 1313 BCE (Hebrew year 2448). References to other cultures are included to understand the specific references of the topic discussed or to give context to the narrative.

In traditional Jewish thought, which provided the basis of the Christian and Islamic religions, monotheism was regarded as its most basic belief. Judaism and Islam have traditionally attempted to interpret scripture as exclusively monotheistic whilst Christianity adopts Trinitarianism, a more complex form of monotheism, as a result of considering the Holy Spirit to be God, and attributing divinity to Jesus, a Judean Jew, in the first century CE, defining him as the Son of God. Thus, "Father, Son and Holy Spirit".

Monotheism in the Hebrew Bible

Further information: God of Israel, Yahweh, and Elohim

The concept of monotheism develops gradually throughout the various books of the Hebrew Bible.

In the oldest sections - some of the Psalms, for example - Yahweh, the God of Israel, is shown as a member of a larger divine council of which El is the head; by the time of the Torah, written most probably around 700-450 BC, Yahweh reveals himself as the national deity to be worshipped alone, but without excluding the existence of other gods. Besides the unambiguous presence of monolatrism by the early 6th century (the late monarchic period), there are some passages in the Hebrew Bible which have also been taken to express monotheism proper, such as Isaiah 44:6,

> "Thus says the LORD, the King of Israel and his Redeemer, the LORD of hosts: "I am the first and I am the last; besides me there is no god"

or Deuteronomy 4:39 ,

> "Know this day, and take it to heart, that the LORD is God in heaven above and on earth below; there is none else."

In the classical interpretation of the Hebrew Bible, as taught in Rabbinical Judaism as well as in Christianity, it was Abraham who discovered God (Genesis 12:1-9; 13:14-18; 1518; and thus became "the world's first monotheist". This is in agreement with the teaching of Islam, holding Abraham to be the original *hanif* (to incline towards a right state).

Rabbinical Judaism

Further information: Judaism

The best-known Jewish statements of monotheism occur in the Shema prayer, the Ten Commandments and Maimonides' 13 Principles of faith, Second Principle:

God, the Cause of all, is one. This does not mean one as in one of a pair, nor one like a species (which encompasses many individuals), nor one as in an object that is made up of many elements, nor as a single simple object that is infinitely divisible. Rather, God is a unity unlike any other possible unity. This is referred to in the Torah (Deuteronomy 6:4): "Hear Israel, the LORD is our God, the LORD is one."

There has historically been disagreement between the Hasidic Jews and the Mitnagdim Jews on various Jewish philosophical issues surrounding certain concepts of monotheism. A similar situation of differing views is seen in modern times among Dor Daim, students of the Rambam, segments of Lithuanian Jewry, and portions of the Modern Orthodox world toward Jewish communities that are more thoroughly influenced by Lurianic Kabbalistic teachings such as Hasidism and large segments of the Sepharadi and Mizrahi communities. This dispute is likely rooted in the differences between what are popularly referred to as the "philosophically inclined" sources and the "kabbalistic sources;" the "philosophic sources" include such Rabbis as Saadia Gaon, Rabenu Bahya ibn Paquda, Abraham ibn Ezra, and Maimonides. The "kabbalistic sources" include Rabbis such as Nahmanides, Bahya ben Asher, Rabbi Yitzhak Saggi Nehor, and Azriel. The Vilna Gaon is usually granted great respect in modern times by those who side with both views; by the more kabbalistic segments of Judaism he is regarded as a great kabbalist; those who take the other side of the issue regard him as a strict advocate of the people of Israel's historical monotheism.

The Shema

Judaism's earliest history, beliefs, laws, and practices are preserved and taught in the Torah (the Hebrew Bible) which provides a clear textual source for the rise and development of what is named Judaism's ethical monotheism which means that:

> *(1) There is one God from whom emanates one morality for all humanity. (2) God's primary demand of people is that they act decently toward one another...The God of ethical monotheism is the God first revealed to the world in the Hebrew Bible. Through it, we can establish God's four primary characteristics:*

1. God is supernatural.
2. God is personal.
3. God is good.
4. God is holy.

> *...in the study of Hebrew history: Israel's monotheism was an ethical monotheism.* Dennis Prager

When Moses returned with the Ten Commandments, the second of those stated that "you shall have no other gods before me" (Exodus 20:3), right after the first, which affirmed the existence of God. Furthermore, Israelites recite the Shema Yisrael ("Hear, O Israel") which partly says, "Hear, O Israel: The Lord our God, the Lord is one." Monotheism was and is the central tenet of the Israelite and the Jewish religion.

The Shema

Hebrew	שמע ישראל יי אלהנו יי אחד
Common transliteration	Shema Yisrael Adonai Eloheinu Adonai Echad
English	Hear, O Israel! The LORD is our God! The LORD is One!

The literal word meanings are roughly as follows:

- Shema — 'listen' or 'hear.' The word also implies comprehension.
- Yisrael — 'Israel', in the sense of the people or congregation of Israel
- Adonai — often translated as 'Lord', it is used in place of the **Tetragrammaton**
- Eloheinu — 'our God', a plural noun (said to imply majesty rather than plural number) with a pronominal suffix ('our')
- Echad — 'one'

In this case, *Elohim* is used in the plural as a form of respect and not polytheism.

Gen.1:26 And Elohim said, Let *us* make man in *our* image, after *our* likeness: and let them have dominion over the fish of the sea, and over the fowl of the air, and over the cattle, and over all the earth, and over every creeping thing that creepeth upon the earth.

Elohim is morphologically plural in form in Hebrew, but generally takes singular agreement when it refers to the God of Israel (so the verb meaning "said" in this verse is *vayyomer* ,noitcelfni ralugnis htiw ויאמר and not *vayyomru* eht esac siht ni tey dna ,(noitcelfni larulp htiw ויאמרו "our" and "us" seems to create a presumption of plurality, though it may just be God talking to angels and not another god.

Judaism, however, insists that the "LORD is One," as in the Shema, and at least two interpretations exist to explain the Torah's use of the plural form. The first is that the plural form "Elohim" is analogous to the royal plural as used in English. The second is that, in order to set an example for human kings, Elohim consulted with his court (the angels, just created) before making a major decision (creating man).

Christian view

Most Christian churches teach the Trinity, an idea which does not conform to unitarian monotheistic beliefs. Historically, most Christian churches have taught that the nature of God is a *mystery*, in the original, technical meaning; something that must be revealed by special revelation rather than deduced through general revelation. Among early Christians there was considerable debate over the nature of godhead, with some factions arguing for the deity of Jesus and others calling for a unitarian conception of God. These issues of Christology were to form one of the main subjects of contention at the First Council of Nicaea.

The **First Council of Nicaea**, held in Nicaea in Bithynia (in present-day Turkey), convoked by the Roman Emperor Constantine I in 325, was the first ecumenical conference of bishops of the Christian Church, and most significantly resulted in the first uniform Christian doctrine, called the Nicene Creed. With the creation of the creed, a precedent was established for subsequent 'general (ecumenical) councils of bishops' (synods) to create statements of belief and canons of doctrinal orthodoxy— the intent being to define unity of beliefs for the whole of Christendom.

The purpose of the council was to resolve disagreements in the Church of Alexandria over the nature of Jesus in relationship to the Father; in particular, whether Jesus was of the same substance as God the Father or merely of similar substance. St. Alexander of Alexandria and Athanasius took the first position; the popular presbyter Arius, from whom the term Arian controversy comes, took the second. The council decided against the Arians overwhelmingly. (Of the estimated 250-318 attendees, all but 2 voted against Arius).

Christian orthodox traditions (Eastern Orthodox, Roman Catholic, Protestant, and Evangelical) follow this decision, which was codified in 381 and reached its full development through the work of the Cappadocian Fathers. They consider God to be a triune entity, called the Trinity, comprising the three "Persons" God the Father, God the

154

Son, and God the Holy Spirit, the three of this unity are described as being "of the same substance" (ὁμοούσιος). The true nature of an infinite God, however, is asserted to be beyond definition, and "the word 'person' is but an imperfect expression of the idea, and is not biblical. In common parlance it denotes a separate rational and moral individual, possessed of self-consciousness, and conscious of his identity amid all changes. Experience teaches that where you have a person, you also have a distinct individual essence. Every person is a distinct and separate individual, in whom human nature is individualized. But in God there are no three individuals alongside of, and separate from, one another, but only personal self distinctions within the divine essence, which is not only generically, but also numerically, one." Some criticscontend that because of the adoption of a tripartite conception of deity, Christianity is actually a form of Tritheism or Polytheism. This concept dates from the teachings of the Alexandrian Church, which claimed that Jesus, having appeared later in the Bible than his "Father," had to be a secondary, lesser, and therefore "distinct" God. This controversy led to the convention of the Nicaean council in 325 CE. For Jews and Muslims, the idea of God as a trinity is heretical—— it is considered akin to polytheism. Christians overwhelmingly assert that monotheism is central to the Christian faith, as the Nicene Creed (and others), which gives the orthodox Christian definition of the Trinity, begins: "I believe in one God".

Some Christians eschew mainstream trinitarian theology; such as the Jehovah's Witnesses, Mormonism, the Unitarians, Christadelphians, Church of God General Conference), Socinian; and some of the Radical Reformers (Anabaptists) do not teach the doctrine of the Trinity at all. The Oneness Pentecostals believe the doctrine of the Trinity is not orthodox theology, and they adhere to the teachings of the Apostles from the times of the New Testament writings before the Council of Nicaea, which taught that God is a Spirit and is one, and Jesus was the visible manifestation of that Spirit.

155

Islamic view

Main articles: *Tawhid and Hanif*

The holy book of Islam, the Qur'an, asserts the existence of a single and absolute truth that transcends the world; a unique and indivisible being who is independent of the creation.[16] The indivisibility of Allah (God) implies the indivisibility of Allah's sovereignty which in turn leads to the conception of the universe as just, coherent and moral rather than as an existential and moral chaos (as in polytheism). Similarly the Qur'an rejects the binary modes of thinking such as the idea of a duality of God by arguing that both good and evil generate from God's creative act and that evil forces have no power to create anything. Allah in Islam is a universal god rather than a local, tribal or parochial one; an absolute who integrates all affirmative values and brooks no evil.

Tawhid constitutes the foremost article of the Muslim profession.[To attribute divinity to a created entity is the only unpardonable sin mentioned in the Qur'an. Muslims believe that the entirety of the Islamic teaching rests on the principle of Tawhid (Oneness of God).

[Bahá'í view

Main article: *God in the Bahá'í Faith*

The Oneness of God is one of the core teachings of the Bahá'í Faith. Bahá'ís believe that there is one supernatural being, God, who has created all existence. God is described as "a personal God, unknowable, inaccessible, the source of all Revelation, eternal, omniscient, omnipresent and almighty."

Bahá'ís believe that although people have different concepts of God and his nature, and call him by different names, everyone is speaking of the same entity. God is taught to be a personal god in that God is conscious of his creation and has a mind, will and purpose. At the same time the Bahá'í teachings state that God is too great for humans to fully understand him or to create a complete and accurate image of him. Bahá'u'lláh teaches that human knowledge of God is limited to those

156

attributes and qualities which are understandable to us, and thus direct knowledge about the essence of God is not possible. Bahá'ís believe, thus, that through daily prayer, meditation, and study of revealed text they can grow closer to God. The obligatory prayers in the Bahá'í Faith involve explicit monotheistic testimony.

Chinese view

Shang Dynasty bronze script character for *tian* (天), which translates to Heaven and sky.
Main articles: Shangdi, Tian, and Mohism

The orthodox faith system held by most dynasties of China since at least the Shang Dynasty (1766 BC) until the modern period centered on the worship of *Shangdi* (literally "Above Sovereign", generally translated as "God") or Heaven as an omnipotent force. This faith system pre-dated the development of Confucianism and Taoism and the introduction of Buddhism and Christianity. It has features of monotheism in that Heaven is seen as an omnipotent entity, endowed with personality but no corporeal form. From the writings of Confucius in the *Analects*, we find that Confucius himself believed that Heaven cannot be deceived, Heaven guides people's lives and maintains a personal relationship with them, and that Heaven gives tasks for people to fulfill in order to teach them of virtues and morality. However, this faith system was not truly monotheistic since other lesser gods and spirits, which varied with locality, were also worshiped along with *Shangdi*. Still, variants such as Mohism approached high monotheism, teaching that the function of lesser gods and ancestral spirits is merely to carry out the will of *Shangdi*, akin to angels in Western civilization. In Mozi's *Will of Heaven* (天志), he writes:

"I know Heaven loves men dearly not without reason. Heaven ordered the sun, the moon, and the stars to enlighten and guide them. Heaven ordained the four seasons, Spring, Autumn, Winter, and Summer, to regulate them. Heaven sent down snow, frost, rain, and dew to grow the five grains and flax and silk that so the people could use and enjoy them. Heaven established the hills and rivers, ravines and valleys, and arranged many things to minister to man's good or bring him evil. He appointed the dukes and lords to reward the virtuous and punish the wicked, and to gather metal and wood, birds and beasts, and to engage in cultivating the five grains and flax and silk to provide for the people's food and clothing. This has been so from antiquity to the present."

Worship of *Shangdi* and Heaven in ancient China includes the erection of shrines, the last and greatest being the Temple of Heaven in Beijing, and the offering of prayers. The ruler of China in every Chinese dynasty would perform annual sacrificial rituals to *Shangdi*, usually by slaughtering a completely healthy bull as sacrifice. Although its popularity gradually diminished after the advent of Taoism and Buddhism, among other religions, its concepts remained in use throughout the pre-modern period and have been incorporated in later religions in China, including terminology used by early Christians in China.

Indian religions

Hinduism

In Hinduism, views are broad and range from monism, pantheism to panentheism – alternatively called monistic theism by some scholars – to monotheism (also see Hindu denominations). Hinduism is often misrepresented as polytheistic.

Rig Veda 1.164.46,

> *Indram mitram varuṇamaghnimāhuratho divyaḥ sa suparṇo gharutmān,*
> *ekam sad viprā bahudhā vadantyaghnim yamam mātariśvānamāhuḥ*
> "They call him Indra, Mitra, Varuṇa, Agni, and he is heavenly nobly-winged Garutmān.
> To what is One, sages give many a title they call it Agni, Yama, Mātariśvan."(trans. Griffith)

158

Vaishnavism is one of the earliest implicit manifestations of monotheism in the traditions of Vedas. *Svayam Bhagavan* is a Sanskrit term for the original deity of the Supreme God worshiped across many traditions of the Vaishnavism, the monotheistic absolute deity. This term is often applied to Krishna in some branches of Vaishnavism. Traditions of Gaudiya Vaishnavas, the Nimbarka Sampradaya and followers of Swaminarayan and Vallabha considers him to be the source of all avataras, and the source of Vishnu himself, or to be the same as Narayana. As such, he is therefore regarded as *Svayam Bhagavan*.

When Krishna is recognized to be *Svayam Bhagavan*, it can be understood that this is the belief of Gaudiya Vaishnavism, the Vallabha Sampradaya, and the Nimbarka Sampradaya, where Krishna is accepted to be the source of all other avatars, and the source of Vishnu himself. This belief is drawn primarily "from the famous statement of the Bhagavatam"1.3.28). A different viewpoint differing from this theological concept is the concept of Krishna as an *avatara* of Narayana or Vishnu. It should be however noted that although it is usual to speak of Vishnu as the source of the avataras, this is only one of the names of the God of Vaishnavism, who is also known as Narayana, Vasudeva and Krishna and behind each of those names there is a divine figure with attributed supremacy in Vaishnavism.

The Rig Veda, the very first book, discusses monotheistic thought. So does Atharva Veda and Yajur Veda."The One Truth, sages know by many names" (Rig Veda 1.164.46)"When at first the unborn sprung into being, He won His own dominion beyond which nothing higher has been in existence" (Atharva Veda 10.7.31)

"There is none to compare with Him. There is no parallel to Him, whose glory, verily, is great." (Yajur Veda 32.3)

The number of auspicious qualities of God are countless, with the following six qualities being the most important:

- *Jñāna* (Omniscience), defined as the power to know about all beings simultaneously

- *Aishvarya* (Sovereignty, derived from the word Ishvara), which consists in unchallenged rule over all
- *Shakti* (Energy), or power, which is the capacity to make the impossible possible
- *Bala* (Strength), which is the capacity to support everything by will and without any fatigue
- *Vīrya* (Vigor), which indicates the power to retain immateriality as the supreme being in spite of being the material cause of mutable creations
- *Tejas* (Splendor), which expresses His self-sufficiency and the capacity to overpower everything by His spiritual effulgence[37]

In the Shaivite tradition, the **Shri Rudram** (Sanskrit श्रि रुद्रम्), to which the Chamakam (चमकम्) is added by scriptural tradition, is a Hindu stotra dedicated to Rudra (an epithet of Shiva), taken from the Yajurveda (TS 4.5, 4.7). Shri Rudram is also known as *Sri Rudraprasna*, *Śatarudrīya*, and *Rudradhyaya*. The text is important in Vedanta where Shiva is equated to the Universal supreme God. The hymn is an early example of enumerating the names of a deity,[1] a tradition developed extensively in the sahasranama literature of Hinduism.

The Nyaya school of Hinduism has made several arguments regarding a monotheistic view. The Naiyanikas have given an argument that such a god can only be one. In the *Nyaya Kusumanjali*, this is discussed against the proposition of the Mimamsa school that let us assume there were many demigods (devas) and sages (rishis) in the beginning, who wrote the Vedas and created the world. Nyaya says that:

[If they assume such] omniscient beings, those endowed with the various superhuman faculties of assuming infinitesimal size, and so on, and capable of creating everything, then we reply that the *law of parsimony* bids us assume only one such, namely Him, the adorable Lord. There can be no confidence in a non-eternal and non-omniscient being, and hence it follows that according to the system which rejects God, the tradition of the Veda is simultaneously overthrown; there is no other way open.

160

In other words, Nyaya says that the polytheist would have to give elaborate proofs for the existence and origin of his several celestial spirits, none of which would be logical, and that it is more logical to assume one eternal, omniscient god.

Sikhism

Sikhism is a monotheistic faith that arose in northern India during the 16th and 17th centuries. Sikhs believe in one, timeless, omnipresent, supreme creator. The opening verse of the Guru Granth Sahib, known as the Mool Mantra signifies this:

"There is only one creator god"

It is often said that the 1430 pages of the Sri Guru Granth Sahib are all expansions on the Mool Mantra. Although the Sikhs have many names for God some of which have derived from Hinduism and Islam, they all refer to the same supreme being. The Islamic holy saints and Hindu saints are revered in high esteem and there teachings are mostly followed and recited during the Sikh prayers.

The Sikh holy scriptures refer to the One God who pervades the whole of space and is the creator of all beings in the universe. The following quotation from the Guru Granth Sahib highlights this point:

"Chant, and meditate on **the One God, who permeates and pervades the many beings of the whole Universe.** God created it, and God spreads through it everywhere. Everywhere I look, I see God. The Perfect Lord is perfectly pervading and permeating the water, the land and the sky; there is no place without Him."
—Guru Granth Sahib, Page 782

However there is a strong case for arguing that the Guru Granth Sahib teaches monism due to its non-dualistic tendencies:

> English: *You have thousands of Lotus Feet, and yet You do not have even one foot. You have no nose, but*

161

*you have thousands of noses. This Play of Yours
entrances me.*

Sikhs believe that God has been given many names, but they all refer to
the One God VāhiGurū. The word Guru means teacher in Sanskrit.
Sikhs believe that members of other religions such as Islam, Hinduism
and Christianity all worship the same god, and the names Allah, Rahim,
Karim, Hari, Raam and Paarbrahm are frequently mentioned in the Sikh
holy scriptures. The Sikh reference to God is Akal Purakh (which
means "the true immortal") or Waheguru, the primal being.

Zoroastrianism

A Zoroastrian is an adherent to Zoroastrianism, a monotheistic religion
which was once one of the biggest religions on Earth, founded in the
early part of the 12-10th century BCE, or possibly even earlier in the
18th Century BCE. The religion is based on the teachings and
philosophies of Zoroaster. The Zoroastrians (or "Parsis") are sometimes
credited with being the first monotheists and having had significant
influence in the formation of current, larger world religions. Today,
some figures put the number of adherents to Zoroastrianism at up to 3.5
million, ranging from regions in South Asia and spread across the
globe.

CPSIA information can be obtained at www.ICGtesting.com
Printed in the USA
LVOW04s0431010914

401800LV00016B/1259/P

9 781453 764619